Touring C. S. Lewis'

Ireland & England

Touring
C. S. Lewis'
Ireland & England

Perry C. Bramlett
Ronald W. Higdon

Maps by Claudia Wells

SMYTH&HELWYS
PUBLISHING INCORPORATED · MACON, GEORGIA

ISBN 1-57312-191-6

Touring C. S. Lewis' Ireland & England

Perry C. Bramlett
Ronald W. Higdon

Copyright © 1998
Smyth & Helwys

6316 Peake Road
Macon, Georgia 31210-3960
1-800-747-3016

Library of Congress Cataloging-in-Publication Data

Bramlett, Perry C.
    Touring C. S. Lewis' Ireland & England/
    Perry C. Bramlett.
    p. cm.
    ISBN 1-57312-191-6   (alk. paper)
1. Lewis, C. S. (Clive Staples), 1898–1963— Homes and haunts
—Ireland—Guidebooks. 2. Lewis, C. S. (Clive Staples), 1898–
1963—Homes and haunts—England—Guidebooks. 3. Lewis, C.
S. (Clive Staples), 1898–1963—Homes and haunts—Northern
Ireland—Guidebooks. 4. Literary landmarks—Northern Ireland
—Guidebooks. 5. Authors, English—20th century—Biography.
6. Literary landmarks—Ireland—Guidebooks. 7. Literary land-
marks—England—Guidebooks. I. Title.
PR6023.E926Z587   1998
823'.912—dc21
[B]   98-24456
                                                        CIP

Contents

Preface

The popularity of C. S. Lewis is greater now than ever. More than 200 million of his books in 30 languages have been sold; English titles average well over 1,000,000 a year in sales. His books are read and taught all over the world, from seminaries and colleges to high schools and middle and even grammar schools. In addition to works written *by* Lewis, more than 120 books have been written *about* him, and 30-40 more will be published before the year 2000. There are 200-plus Lewis societies and reading groups of all types around the world, and this number is increasing.

Lewis' life and works are recorded on videotape, audiotape, compact disk, and laser disk. The movie *Shadowlands* was produced by the BBC in 1985 and televised nationally on CBS and PBS. In 1993, Richard Attenborough directed it as a major motion picture starring Anthony Hopkins and Debra Winger. In addition, productions of *Shadowlands*, the Narnian tales, *The Screwtape Letters*, *A Grief Observed*, and others are performed every year in colleges, churches, and amateur playhouses, and in off-Broadway and other professional productions.

Interest in C. S. Lewis extends to the places he knew so well: Ireland and England. In celebration of the centenary of Lewis' birth, 1998 will be a tour-filled year. The C. S. Lewis Centenary Group of Ireland is sponsoring several tours ("The C. S. Lewis Trail" and others) of his home, church, and favorite places in and around his birthplace Belfast. There are also many tours originating in the United States sponsored by churches, colleges, and independent Lewis groups.

Many persons have consulted Lewis web pages on the Internet and Lewis organizations for travel ideas and itineraries. They want information about the best known as well as the lesser known places in the life and works of Lewis. They want to know where to go, how to get there, and how to arrange schedules for putting it all together. You have in hand a book that can help you do just that.

This is a book for those planning a tour of the places of C. S. Lewis, a Christian of great ideas and very great faith. It is a unique guide for 1998 and beyond. It presents pieces of geography as seen and experienced by C. S. Lewis. It includes discussions of his homes, churches, colleges, pubs, and favorite places to visit and study, as well as those of his friends, family, and influences. But this book includes more than just geography. It contains the taste, the texture, the tone, and the feel of the life and times of a Christian writer who is now read, studied, and thought about more than ever . . . and for good reason.

In addition to interesting biographical and historical information about people and places associated with C. S. Lewis, this volume includes an annotated bibliography, suggested tours, and relevant maps. The bibliography contains comments on the best and most accessible works about C. S. Lewis and the friends and places in his life. Suggested tours are given for 5 to 10 days and 10 to 20 days, followed by maps of Ireland, Belfast, Oxford, Magdalen College at Oxford, Headington in Oxford, Cambridge, Magdalene College at Cambridge, and England.

Walking in the footsteps of Lewis and his friends provides the opportunity for even greater understanding of who he was and what he had to say. It is the authors' prayer and hope that this book will not only "whet the appetite" of the reader for more of Lewis, but that it will also provide sight and insight for all of those who wish to walk in the world of C. S. Lewis.

We dedicate this volume to our wives, Joan Bramlett and Pat Higdon, both good travelers and exemplary companions. We owe a special thanks to Claudia Wells of Broadway Baptist Church in Louisville, Kentucky, for her splendid drawings of the maps herein. We also express gratitude to Mr. James O'Fee of the Ireland C. S. Lewis Centenary Group. A lifelong resident of County Down, Mr. O'Fee provided valuable information about Lewis' Belfast and the surrounding countryside. Our appreciation also goes to Steve and Angela of Daeron's Books in Milton Keynes, England, and Mr. Phil Salin of the Haunted Bookshop in Cambridge. Mrs. Carol Christman of Evansville, Indiana, gave us some valued and little known information about J. R. R. Tolkien and Bournemouth, and we greatly appreciate her kindness.

Ireland

"All the mountains look like mountains in a story . . ."

Belfast and Environs

C. S. Lewis was born and raised in Belfast. Many of the films and books about him do not mention this fact, and overemphasize his "Englishness" and the time he spent in Oxford and Cambridge. But Lewis often said and wrote that his childhood and early teenage years in Ireland were among the happiest of his whole life. He always treasured his Irish history and heritage, and visited Ireland as often as his busy schedule would allow.

Belfast is located in the northeast corner of Ireland, and sits on an inlet of the Irish Sea, Belfast Lough, at the mouth of the Lagan River, ringed by the mountains of the river valley. It is the second largest city in Ireland, with a population of more than 500,000 in the urban area. In Lewis' time (1898-1917), more than 300,000 people lived in Belfast.

Belfast is a delightful and charming city to visit. It is safe for the visitor and tourist, in fact, much safer than most major European and North American cities. Belfast's crime rate is very low. Even during the recent "Troubles," no American or foreign visitor has been harmed. The visitor to the city can easily avoid areas that have been scarred by violence—these are well known and often marked—or drive through them. Whatever the choice, the visitor to Belfast will be safe. Eastern Belfast, around the Lewis sites, is normally very quiet.

The Lewis sites in Belfast are in the eastern section of the city, in the district called Strandtown. Following is a listing and commentary on the places in Ireland that were especially dear to Lewis.

Homes

Dundela Villas—The birthplace of C. S. (29 November 1898) and Warren Lewis (16 June 1895), and the Lewis family home from the late 1800s till 1905. Lewis' father Albert never owned the Villas; they were rented to him by Thomas Keown (1860-1935), the Belfast banker who built them and who later married Albert's older sister Sara Jane Lewis. C. S. Lewis said that his memories of childhood and living at Dundela Villas were dominated by "good parents, good food, a garden, his nurse Lizzie Endicott, and his brother."

The home was one of a pair of semidetached houses located on 47 Dundela Avenue in the suburb or area called "Dundela," the larger district of Strandtown, about 2 miles from the Belfast City centre. It was probably built in the 1850s and originally adjoined a coach house. The Villas were demolished in 1952 and replaced by Dundela Flats, a "subdivision" of apartments and small homes.

To locate Dundela Flats, from the northern city centre travel east over the River Lagan, which intersects the city north to south, via the Queen's Bridge. This becomes Newtownards Road, a well-known west-east thoroughfare. Continue for several miles to Holywood Road, a left exit traveling northeast. After a few miles, look for Dundela Avenue on the right.

Leeborough House ("Little Lea")—The Lewis family home from 1905 to 1930. C. S., or "Jack," as he was called by family and friends, lived here till about 1917. Located at 76 Circular Road in Strandtown, about 2 miles from Dundela Villas near what is now Craigavon Hospital, Little Lea was built by Albert Lewis, and the family spent their first night here on 21 April 1905. At that time the house was in open countryside on the outskirts of Belfast, but it is now surrounded by residences, roads, and businesses.

Little Lea is a large brick and stucco house, 3 stories high, having chimneys and large bay windows, with the front door and entrance porch at the back of the house away from the street. In his autobiography *Surprised By Joy*, Lewis wrote of his new home: "I am the product of long corridors, empty sunlit rooms, upstairs indoor silences, attics explored in solitude, distant noises of gurgling cisterns and pipes, and the noise of the wind under the tiles."

Due in part to the inclement Irish weather, Jack and Warren often had to stay indoors at Little Lea. Here they would write, play games, draw, and make up imaginary worlds. Later, some of these worlds were captured in *Boxen*, a volume of animal stories (with illustrations) that was published after Jack's death in 1963. Jack and Warren's mother Flora died of cancer at Little Lea in 1908, when Jack was 9 years old and Warren was 12.

To locate Little Lea, follow Holywood Road north, then turn right on Circular Road. The house is about halfway around the circle past Cairnburn Road on the right. On the right side of the house facing the street, on the second level, there is a round commemorative marker that reads:

Ulster History Circle C. S. Lewis 1898-1963 Author and Critic lived here 1905-1917.

Family, Friends, Influences

Bernagh—Where Jack wrote *The Pilgrim's Regress* (1933), his first book as a Christian. Located across the street from Little Lea (109 Circular Road), this was the home of the Greeves family. The youngest of the 5 boys in the family was named Arthur (born 1895), and he and Jack first met in April 1914. Arthur was a lonely boy with a weak heart who had tried several times to get to know the Lewis brothers. When he and Jack met and began an immediate and lifelong friendship, they discovered they had many things in common, particularly a love for Norse mythology and literature.

Arthur was Jack's second great friend, next only to his brother Warren, and they remained friends for nearly half a century. Arthur and Jack wrote regular letters, and each visited the other often in their later lives. On his annual summer holidays in Ireland, Lewis would always spend time with Arthur, and Greeves visited him several times in Oxford. Several hundred of Jack's letters to Arthur survive. In 1979, they were published as *They Stand Together—The Letters of C. S. Lewis to Arthur Greeves (1914–1963)*. Today Bernagh is called "Red Hall," and is a private nursing home.

Cottage 21, Ballymullan Road, Crawfordsburn—A cottage in the Silver Hill district where Arthur Greeves moved in 1949. Crawfordsburn is a picturesque little village (population 500) about 20 miles from Little Lea, between Holywood and (2 miles west of) Bangor, straight northeast on the A2 road, which runs along the coastline of the Irish Sea. During Jack's summer holidays, Arthur often drove him (Jack never learned to drive) to this area of Northern Ireland.

The Old Inn, Crawfordsburn—After 1949, where Jack usually spent the first week of his holiday. It is an early 17th-century inn a few minutes walk from Arthur Greeves' home in Silver Hill, to the right and east down Ballymullan Road. The Old Inn claims to be the oldest Inn in Ireland, with records dating back to 1614. Some of its more notable guests have included Tsar Peter the Great of Russia, legendary highway man Dick Turpin, and former U.S. President George Bush. In 1958, Lewis took his new wife Joy to spend a belated honeymoon at the Old Inn. They lived in the Pantiles bungalow at the back of the inn, now known as the Garden Cottage. They were able to return to the Old Inn in June 1959 for a week's holiday and a visit with Greeves.

21 Eliza Street—The home of Arthur T. Kirkpatrick, Lewis' tutor and one of his greatest influences. This house was located in the "Markets" area of Belfast, near the city centre and west of the river Lagan. According to the Ireland Lewis Centenary Group, "pensioners cottages" stand where Kirkpatrick's Victorian home once was.

For further information on Kirkpatrick, see Royal Belfast Academical Institution (see p. 10), Lurgan College (see p. 9), Queen's University (see p. 10), and Great Bookham, Surrey (see p. 85).

Glenmachan—Home of Jack and Warnie's neighbors the Ewarts, who were cousins of Flora Lewis and wealthy Belfast linen manufacturers. The Ewart family lived at this home (now demolished; modern housing covers the site), which is close to Little Lea, at the top of Cairnburn Road near Glenmachen Drive. The Ewarts were members of St. Mark's church (see p. 8) and, in 1901, built the chancel and transepts for the church.

As a teenager, Jack developed a crush on one of the Ewart girls, Grundeda, and called her the most beautiful woman he had ever seen, with a "radiant and infectious childlike gaiety." Grundeda and her two sisters, Hope and Kelsie, often visited Little Lea and played with the Lewis brothers, and had tennis parties at Glenmachen for other family members, Arthur Greeves, Jack, and Warnie.

In *Surprised By Joy*, Lewis called Glenmachan "Mountbracken," no doubt to insure the Ewart family's privacy. A nursing home (formerly a hotel) called "Glenmachan Tower" standing near this site also has a connection to Lewis. In a letter to Arthur Greeves dated 3 March 1963, just a few months before his death, Lewis mentioned a future meeting at the Glenmachan Tower Hotel and asked Arthur if he could accompany him and his stepson Douglas on a holiday.

Lisnadene House—Home of Janie McNeill (1889–1959), a lifelong friend of the Lewis brothers. Janie was born at 3 West Elmwood, Belfast, and lived at this Victorian home at 191 Belmont Road, Strandtown, close to Belmont Presbyterian church, about 1/2 mile from Little Lea. The house has sadly been demolished in favor of 4 inferior modern dwellings. It is interesting to note that Jack not only dedicated his space novel *That Hideous Strength* (1945) to Janie, but also named one its major characters "Jane" (Studdock). Warren Lewis dedicated one of his French history books, *The Sunset of the Splendid Century*, to Janie. A very strong-willed and vibrant personality, Janie told a friend that she hated being mentioned in *That Hideous Strength* and wished "he'd dedicated any book other than that one to me!"

Ty-Issa—Home of Jack and Warnie's paternal grandfather, Richard Lewis II, who moved to Belfast from Dublin in 1868. There he took a job as a partner in a shipbuilding company, and after the business prospered, moved from the Mount Pottinger area of Belfast to Lower Sydenham. There he bought Ty-Issa ("the house alone"), which still stands. Ty-Issa was only recently discovered by the Ireland Centenary Group, and has changed very little.

To reach Ty-Issa, vear toward the Belfast city centre on Holywood Road, and look for Parkgate Avenue on the right. Ty-Issa, complete with a beautiful red door, is located on Parkgate Avenue near St. Mark's church and the Holywood Road branch library.

Westlands—The former home of Tom Greeves, Arthur's older brother. It is located on Maxwell Road, Bangor, 13 miles from the center of Belfast, in the fashionable Princetown area. Lewis and his wife Joy once visited here in the 1950s. Westlands is owned today by a businessman who is a Lewis enthusiast, and one of his employees is the sculptor of the proposed Lewis memorial statue to be placed near Ty-Issa, in front of the Holywood branch library.

To reach Bangor from St. Mark's Church (see p. 8), follow Holywood Road northeast. Bangor is a few miles north of Crawfordsburn and is located on the Irish Sea, about 15 miles from Strandtown. It has a population of about 45,000, more than twice the number in Lewis' day.

Other Places of Interest

Harland and Wolff Shipbuilding Company—Owned the shipyards where the famous vessels *Olympic* and *Titanic* were built. The Harland and Wolff company survives today on the same site and in the same business, though with a much reduced workforce. Little Lea, the Lewis family home, overlooked the Belfast Lough and the shipyards. Lewis mentioned early in *Surprised By Joy* that in his child-hood the Lough "was full of shipping" and a "delight to us boys."

Work began on the *Olympic* on 16 December 1908, and on the *Titanic* in late 1909. The Lewis brothers delighted in the "busyness" of the Lough's shipping industry and most likely watched from the windows of Little Lea the progress of the construction of the two ships. The *Olympic* was launched on 20 October 1910, and left Belfast Lough on 31 May 1911. The *Titanic* was launched a few hours before the *Olympic*'s departure, and left Belfast Lough forever on 2 April 1912 for Southampton and the start of her ill-fated and now world-famous maiden voyage.

In chapter 10 of *Surprised By Joy*, Lewis wrote of the continual noise of Belfast (locally called "the Belfast Symphony") as being dominated by "the continual throb and stammer of the great shipyards." For Lewis, the "Symphony" was not disconcerting: "It does not . . . violate the peace of the hilltop; rather it emphasizes it." Lewis enrolled in Cherbourg House, Malvern, England, in January 1911, and although he doubtless followed the news of the ship's construction via letters from home and occasional visits, he probably missed the *Titanic's* final departure.

Churches

Glencraig Parish Church—A church on the main road near Holywood, about 5 miles northeast of Strandtown, where Lewis once worshiped in the 1950s. In his day it was the mother church of St. John's, Helen's Bay.

To reach the church from Little Lea, follow Cairnburn Road east to Old Holywood Road, turn left, and travel north a few miles toward Holywood.

Glencraig New Vicarage—A house located on the site of the Old Vicarage, where the wife of the former Vicar, Mrs. Hill, once entertained Lewis after a worship service. Mrs. Hill is still alive, and has mentioned Lewis' visit to the Lewis Centenary Group.

Parish Rectory, Glencraig Church—Visited by Lewis as a boy, according to the Ireland C. S. Lewis Centenary Group.

St. Mark's Church, Dundela—C. S. Lewis' "home church," where he was baptized (29 January 1899) at the font at the west end of the church and confirmed (6 December 1914). In Lewis' day, the church's membership was about 300 families; today its congregation numbers about 800 families.

St. Mark's was established in 1874, and Lewis' grandfather Thomas Hamilton (1826–1905) was its first rector, serving from 1874 till 1900. Lewis' father Albert served as a churchwarden at St. Mark's and was the church's first Sunday School Superintendent. The silver vessels still used for communion and the brass lectern were donated by Albert and his brothers and sisters. It was at St. Mark's that Albert met and later married Flora Hamilton on 29 August 1894.

When Albert died in 1929, Jack had become a professor at Oxford University, and his brother Warren was a career army officer. In 1932, Jack and Warnie presented a stained glass window to St. Mark's in memory of their parents. The Lewis Window, designed by the noted Dublin artist Michael Healy, may be seen today on the south side of the church, second from the back on the right hand side. Saints Luke, James, and Mark are represented in the window. Translated, the Latin text under the window reads:

> To the greater glory of God and dedicated to the memory of Albert James Lewis, who died on the 25th September 1929, aged 67, and also of his wife, Flora Augusta Hamilton, who died on the 23rd August 1908, aged 47.

To visit St. Mark's, go from the city centre over the River Lagan via the Queen's Bridge and on to Newtownards Road. Then find Holywood Road (left). Travel northeast past Belmont Road on the right (Pimms Avenue is on the left) to the church, which is on the right, just past Sydenham Road on the left. If necessary, call the Lewis Centenary Group at Belfast for directions (672351; first dial 01232 if calling long distance) .

The Old Rectory, St. Mark's—The former home of Lewis' grandfather Thomas Hamilton, who lived here when he was rector. This house faces Holywood Road on the Belfast Side of St. Mark's Church, on the same site. The Ireland Lewis Centenary Group newsletter is posted and E-mailed from the house by the Church of Ireland Ace Ventures, one of the current occupants.

The New Rectory, St. Mark's—Home of the current Ireland Lewis Centenary Group, it stands near the Old Rectory.

Colleges and Schools

Campbell College—Where C. S. Lewis attended school from September to December 1910 following the closing of Wynyard School (see p. 81), a boy's "prep" school in Watford, Herfordshire. Campbell is about 1 mile from Little Lea. Its first headmaster was James A. McNeill, the father of Lewis' close friend Janie McNeill. A few years after Lewis attended Campbell, William MacQuitty was a student here. MacQuitty later was the producer of the first film about the *Titanic*, entitled *A Night to Remember*, based on the bestselling book by Walter Lord. The Campbell College War Memorial contains the names of pupils who volunteered during World War I, including C. S. Lewis, who was wounded in France in 1918.

To reach Campbell College from Little Lea, from Circular Road go east on Cairnburn Road to Old Holywood Road. From there turn right (south) and go to Belmont Road, and then turn right on Belmont Road, which leads to Campbell on the right.

Lurgan College—A small college located in the city of Lurgan, County Armagh, about 22 miles southwest of Belfast, off the M1 highway. Albert Lewis attended college (secondary school) here from 1877 to 1879. At the age of 14, he began studying under Arthur T. Kirkpatrick, then 31 years of age. Kirkpatrick was Headmaster at Lurgan from 1876 to 1899. These were enjoyable times for Albert, due to the fact that Kirkpatrick, a brilliant scholar, took him under his wing and offered him special advice and encouragement. While at Lurgan, Albert decided to study law—with Kirkpatrick's blessing. "The Great Knock," as the Lewis family called Kirkpatrick, remained a loyal friend and counsel. Because of this friendship, Albert later encouraged his son Jack to study under Kirkpatrick in preparation for Oxford.

Royal Belfast Academical Institution—Popularly known as "Inst," a Presbyterian-affiliated school built in 1814 for the training of medical students. It is considered one of Belfast's finest prep schools. Arthur T. Kirkpatrick taught English at Inst from 1868 to 1876. Located in the left-center of the city on Durham Street near Grosvenor Road, Inst is in short walking distance of the Grand Opera House and City Hall.

Queen's University—Once known as Queen's College, a famous school where both Arthur T. Kirkpatrick and Flora Lewis studied. Kirkpatrick graduated from Queen's in 1868 with honors in English, History, and Metaphysics. In 1870, he received a master's degree. Flora Lewis attended Queen's from 1881 to 1886, gaining honors in Geometry, Algebra, and Mathematics. She is mentioned in *Degrees of Excellence: The Story of Queen's, Belfast 1845–1995* (Brian Walker and Alf McCreary, The Institute of Irish Studies, 1994) as gaining fourth place in the second year examinations and being "recalled with affection in the writings of her son, C. S. Lewis, the famous religious writer and author of children's stories."

The first college in Ireland to admit women, Queen's was built in 1849, and resembles Lewis' Magdalen College, Oxford, in its architecture and Tudor styling. It has an international reputation and is Northern Ireland's most prestigious university. It is located in the southern center of Belfast, about 2 miles from City Hall, on University Road near Botanic Avenue.

Holidays and Walks

C. S. Lewis loved to take walks. He often walked in the area around Little Lea with his brother and other friends. He would often walk along Cairnburn Road, past Janie McNeill's home, Lisnadene. He would also walk into the Holywood Hills past the "Shepherd's Hut," also called "Shepherd's Cot" (cottage), now demolished.

Another favorite walk was to turn left on Old Holywood Road, east from Cairnburn Road, and then travel to the town of Holywood, about 50 minutes and 5 miles. In the 1920s, Jack and Warnie would then turn into the old Central Hotel (later the Belfast Hotel, and today an office building) close to the Holywood Maypole in the center of town for a refreshing pint of beer. The brothers would return to Little Lea by the main Belfast Road and then by Circular Road.

The hills and mountains around Belfast were very dear to Lewis, and he visited them often, especially during his youth. The low ridge of hills to the east of the city is named the Holywood Hills, those north of the Dundonald Gap, which is north of the main Belfast-Newtownards Road, which winds through the Gap. Part of this low ridge is also known as the Castlereagh ("Grey Castle") Hills, those south of the Dundonald Gap. Jack and Warren could easily see these hills from Dundela Villas, and later the Holywood Hills from Little Lea.

In the first chapter of *Surprised By Joy*, Lewis called the Castlereagh Hills "the Green Hills." Later in the book he wrote that they were his "main haunt," and that from them, looking north and east, he could see the "whole expanse of the Lough," the Antrim coast, and on a good day, Scotland could be seen to the west, "phantomlike on the horizon." Looking south, he could stand and see the Plain of Down, and further, the Mourne Mountains.

The Carlingford Mountains in County Louth, across from the Mournes, were very important to Lewis, for this was the region of the country that he thought most resembled the country of Narnia. For Lewis, these views and sights from his early years triggered his imagination and awakened a sense of longing in his heart, which he later called "joy."

Ireland

Holidays and Visits

Ballycastle, County Antrim—A seaside resort north of Belfast where Flora Lewis and a nurse took Warren (age 5) and Jack (age 2) on their first recorded family holiday, 6-27 August 1900. (See Warren Lewis' diary *Brothers and Friends*, 1982). The pretty, small town sits on the coast where the Atlantic Ocean meets the Irish Sea. It still retains much of its 18th- and 19th-century architecture and seaside flavor. Ballycastle is about 55 miles northwest of Belfast, at the very northern tip of County Antrim. It is the home of Ireland's oldest and most popular fair, Ould Lammas, dating from the 1400s.

Castlerock, County Derry—A seasode resort about 30 miles west of Ballycastle where Flora, Warren, and Jack vacationed often. In *Brothers and Friends*, Warren recorded specific holidays the family took to Castlerock in June–July 1901, June–August 1904, and September 1906. The area is known for its beauty and long, sandy beach, and boasts a 17th-century Victorian thatched farmhouse called "Hezlett House," which has long been admired by visitors. The name Castlerock comes from the two huge rocks on the shoreline that stand like turrets on a castle.

Ballynahinch, County Down—Where Flora, Warren, and Jack vacationed at the Spar Hotel in May 1903. Ballynahinch is also the birthplace of Amanda Mc'Kittrick Ros (1860–1939), who is infamous for her reputation as the worst novelist (and poet) of this century. Despite this, Mrs. Ros became something of a cult figure on account of her "gloriously awful" writing, and Aldous Huxley, for one, made strenuous efforts to see that her works remained in print. Both London and Cambridge sponsored clubs where her novels were regularly read and discussed, probably with tongue in cheek. Lewis and the Inklings (see p. 26) would read her *Irene Iddesleigh* (1897) to amuse themselves and to see who could read the longest without breaking up laughing. Ballynahinch is about 13 miles south of Belfast.

Kilkeel, County Down—A resort and fishing town 40 miles south of Belfast near the Mourne Mountains on the Irish Sea where Warnie and Jack Lewis and Mrs. Janie Moore, Jack's "adopted mother," and her daughter Maureen vacationed 29 July 1934. The name Kilkeel means "church of the narrows."

Portsalon, County Donegal—Where Jack Lewis and Arthur Greeves vacationed in August 1916. Portsalon is a tiny village once renowned as a great vacation area, but now virtually abandoned by tourists. It lies about 60 miles northwest of Belfast, on the northeastern side of the Fanod Peninsula, on Ballymastocker Bay. This area of Northern Ireland is known for its idyllic scenery, solitude, and quaint villages and towns.

Rathmullan, County Donegal—Where Lewis and his wife Joy spent some time in the summer of 1959, after a trip to Crawfordsburn and the Old Inn. They stayed at the Royal Fort Hotel, which still exists with its own private beach. Rathmullan is a very old little town, rich in history, and has not changed much over the years. It boasts a 15th-century Carmelite priory and a stunning view across the Mill Bay to Fahan on the Inishowen peninsula. From the Rathmullan pier, an attractive coastal walk leads between private gardens and the shore to a beautiful woodland area. Rathmullan is a few miles south of Portsalon on the R247 road.

Other Places of Interest

Drogheda, County Louth—Location of Our Lady of Lourdes Hospital where, in his later life, Warren Lewis was treated for acute alcoholism. The hospital is located slightly northwest of the river in the center of the city, on Windmill Road. Drogheda is a picturesque and historic town located about 31 miles north of Dublin and 81 miles south of Belfast on the N1 highway. It sits on the River Boyne, about 3 miles from the Irish Sea, and today is one of Ireland's busiest towns, with a population of about 30,000. The town still has a medieval atmosphere with its 13th-century streets and old buildings, including the 1224 Magdalene Tower in the northern part of town.

Cork City, County Cork—Birthplace of Albert Lewis (23 August 1863). The cosmopolitan city of Cork is about 265 miles southwest of Belfast and is Ireland's third largest.

Queenstown, County Cork—Birthplace of Flora Lewis (18 May 1862).

Pomeroy, County Tyrone—Birthplace of Janie King Moore (28 March 1872). Pomeroy is a small village about 12 miles southwest of Cookstown and 33 miles from Belfast. Mrs. Moore grew up in Dunany, County Louth.

Delgany, County Wicklow—Birthplace of Maureen Moore (Blake) (19 August 1906; died 14 February 1997). Delgany is a small village about 12 miles south of Dublin, a short distance to the west of the resort and seacoast town of Greystones. It is noted for its parish church, Christ Church, built on the site of a 7th-century church, and for its 18th-century pubs.

Kingstown, County Dublin—Birthplace of Lewis' friend Edward Francis C. "Paddy" Moore (17 November 1898) (see Bristol, p. 83).

Leighlinbridge, County Carlow—The home of Douglas Gresham, stepson of C. S. Lewis and son of Joy Gresham Lewis. After living for many years in Tasmania, where he was a farmer and radio broadcaster, Mr. Gresham and his wife Merrie moved to Ireland in 1993, where he now works for the C. S. Lewis Estate and supports several other Christian ministries. He is the author of *Lenten Lands* (1988), a memoir about his life with his mother and C. S. Lewis. Leighlinbridge is about 60 miles south of Dublin and boasts one of Ireland's first Norman castles, dating back to 1181. It has the ambiance of an earlier time, with its castle, old malt houses, and river walks.

Skibbereen, County Cork—Birthplace of Lewis' great friend and fellow Inkling (see p. 27) Nevill H. Coghill (19 April 1899). Skibbereen is a thriving market town and popular tourist attraction on the "Cork Trail," and is located about 55 miles southwest of Cork City.

Trinity College, Dublin—Where C. S. Lewis was a guest speaker and lecturer for the Historical Society in the early 1950s. Founded in 1592, Trinity is one of the great seats of learning in the world. It covers 40 acres in the south center of the city and has more than 7,000 students. Trinity lies just below the Iffley River and sits between Pearse Road and Nassau Street.

Oxford

"There was the fabled cluster of spires and towers . . ."

The City of Oxford

Oxford is a city of about 100,000 people, with a history dating back to Saxon times. The first major settlement was located at what is now the site of the 8th-century St. Frideswide Abbey in present-day St. Aldate's. The original "oxen ford," from which the city got its name, was probably at what is now Folly Bridge, and the essential layout of Oxford was established in 901. The core of the city then and now sits on the terrace between the upper Thames

River, known locally as the Isis, and the smaller river Cherwell. Oxford is about 56 miles west by road from London and 80 miles south from Cambridge.

The acclaimed travel writer Jan Morris has observed that "few cities have been more loved, loathed, and celebrated" than Oxford. This is the city that has given the world the MG sports car, 23 British prime ministers, a marmalade, bags, a grey, shoes, a Group, a Movement, a dictionary, and an accent, plus countless famous diplomats, lawyers, scientists, clergy, musicians, poets, writers, and of course C. S. Lewis and the Inklings.

Oxford is more crowded and busier than Cambridge, seems larger than it really is, and can be maddeningly arrogant at times. But like Cambridge, Oxford is a wonderful place for visitors. Along with "Inspector Morse's" pubs and many others, there are dozens of shops (book and others), art and antique galleries, museums, libraries, beautiful old colleges, restaurants and sweets shops, and gardens and parks to spend time in.

The visitor to Oxford can pass the house where Edmund Halley discovered his comet, stroll in the meadow where "Lewis Carroll" worked on his Alice stories, visit the oldest public museum in England (the Ashmolean), and climb the Magdalen Tower where part of *Shadowlands* was filmed. Or, if so inclined, a person can walk through the maze of backlanes that wander around and past the 900-plus historical buildings in central Oxford, or rent a car and drive around and look at the homes of North Oxford, quite possibly England's most eagerly hoped-for residences.

When C. S. Lewis saw Oxford for the first time in early December 1916, he wrote to his father and said that "the place has surpassed my wildest dreams: I never saw anything so beautiful." Much later, in *Surprised By Joy*, he described his comical adventure of getting lost on his first trip to the city, then turning around and looking back at the beauty of "the fabled cluster of spires and towers." For many visitors to Oxford, the magic of "the dreaming spires" sets this wonderful place apart from all the rest. The "oldness" and tradition can be a little overwhelming at first, but after a few days most people usually end up thinking how lucky they are to be there.

Oxford University

Today Oxford University has 30 undergraduate colleges, 9 graduate colleges, and 6 permanent private halls that accommodate a little more than 14,000 students. While the essential appeal of the university is the medieval atmosphere of many of the college "quads," chapels, and grounds, much has changed since the early days, and even from the time when Lewis was here.

In the 19th century, under the guidance of strong-willed men such as John Ruskin and Benjamin Jowett, the University reformed from being a medieval, religious-oriented institution to a modern education-centered establishment devoted to teaching and scholarship, with particular emphasis on the arts and sciences. But the colleges remain as they have always been, self-contained independent corporations with their own laws and ways of doing things. The University is still very proud of its traditions, but have incorporated these into a modern approach to teaching and learning.

Much of the appeal of the University to the visitor lies in the variety of colleges. They range in size from Nuffield, with 75 students, to New, with about 600. The wealthiest colleges—St. John's, Christ Church, and Magdalen—are possibly a hundred times richer than the poorest—Hertford, Keble, St. Edmund Hall, and St. Peter's.

Buildings range from Merton's tiny, medieval Mob Quadrangle to the 18th-century dignity of Magdalen's New Buildings, the wild patterned Victorian brick of Keble, and the concrete and glass modernity of Wolfson. In atmosphere, the colleges range from Christ Church and Magdalen's wide-meadowed, tree-lined stately atmosphere, to Wadham's cosy, casual garden intimacy, and to Balliol and University's rather sophisticated, scholarly attitude. But the visitor to Oxford University will find that most all of its colleges, especially the older ones, have plenty in common.

They all have exquisite gardens, lovely and interesting chapels, quiet walks, beautiful architecture, great traditions and history, famous graduates, interesting people, and a promising future. C. S. Lewis knew this, too. He loved Oxford and was proud of his association with it.

Magdalen College

Lewis was a tutor in the English department of Magdalen College from 1925 to 1954. Magdalen (pronounced "Maudlin") was founded in 1458, and one its first fellows was Thomas Wolsey, who later founded Christ Church. The college was built on the site of the Hospital of St. John the Baptist, some of whose buildings still stand on the college's High Street side.

Being outside the original city walls, Magdalen had plenty of room to grow, and both its quadrangles and grounds are exceptionally spacious. The world-famous Bell Tower, completed between 1492 and 1509, is an Oxford landmark, standing as a sentinel over the Magdalen Bridge to the east. It was one of Lewis' favorite sites at the college, and the "May Day singing scene" in *Shadowlands* (with Anthony Hopkins and Debra Winger) was filmed there.

While at Magdalen, Lewis lived in Rooms 3 on Staircase 3 of New Buildings, built in 1733. On arriving here in October 1925, he wrote to his father, "My external surroundings are beautiful beyond expectation and beyond hope." From his rooms he could see "nothing, not even a gable or spire, to remind me that I am in a town." It was in these rooms that he met students for tutorials and hosted Inklings meetings on Thursday nights for many years.

To the left from New Buildings is Magdalen Grove (not open to the public), where deer have grazed since 1700. To the right of and facing New Buildings, a bridge leads to a meadow by the Cherwell River. This area is enclosed by Addison's Walk, named after Joseph Addison (1672–1719), a well-known poet and essayist and a former fellow at Magdalen. Lewis and his friends strolled along this path many times. It was here on 19 September 1931 that he, J. R. R. Tolkien, and "Hugo" Dyson had their famous "long night walk" and conversation, which led Lewis to belief in the Jesus of the Gospels.

To locate the New Buildings, enter the college on High Street, go through the Porter's Lodge, then take the right side of St. John's Quadrangle to the Chapel entrance (right). From here walk to the far left (north) of the Great Quadrangle and go out a walkway in the middle. The New Buildings are straight ahead across a green. The bridge to Addison's Walk is to the right.

The "angel scene" in the original BBC version of *Shad-owlands*, starring Claire Bloom and Joss Ackland, was filmed in the Magdalen College chapel, where Lewis often worshiped "in term." The chapel was completed around 1480, and the interior was completely renovated and restored between 1828 and 1835. There is a brass memorial to Lewis in the antechapel, and the interior is today as Lewis saw it during his time at Magdalen.

Colleges and Private Halls

Blackfriars—The home of Lewis' friend and Inkling Father Gervase Mathew (1905–1976), who lived here from about 1929 till his death. Father Mathew began attending Ink-lings meetings in 1939, and is first mentioned by Warren Lewis in *Brothers and Friends*. His academic specialty was Byzantine studies. He also lectured at the University in history, theology, and English. He wrote several books about Byzantine life and culture, and contributed an article to *Essays Presented to Charles Williams*, edited by Lewis. He also wrote the essay "Ideals of Friendship" in *Patterns of Love and Courtesy: Essays in Memory of C. S. Lewis* (1966), edited by Lewis' student John Lawlor.

Blackfriars is a Dominican friary founded in 1921 and located in St. Giles next to Pusey House and near the Eagle and Child.

Christ Church—Perhaps the most beautiful and visited college in Oxford, boasting some of the grandest and most stunning architecture in the University. Its Great Quad-rangle, known as Tom Quad, and Hall (115'x40') are the largest in Oxford. Built between 1160 and 1200, its cathedral is the smallest of England's ancient cathedrals. And Christopher Wren's Tom Tower is a symbol of Oxford worldwide.

Locally called "the House," Christ Church is perhaps best known as the home of Charles Ludwig Dodgson ("Lewis Carroll," 1832–1898), a mathematics professor and assistant librarian here from 1855 till his death. Carroll's *Alice in Wonderland* stories have focused much attention on Christ Church, and thousands from all over the world have visited the college in search of Alice sites. Lewis visited the House several times, once to attend a performance of the play *Glorious England* in the Priory Gardens on 31 July 1922. The play was written by Bernice de Bergerac, a friend of Leo Baker, who was an early college friend of Lewis.'

To reach Christ Church from Lewis' Magdalen College, take Rose Lane (left) in front of the Botanic Gardens to Deadman's Walk, which runs parallel to Merton College going west. This leads to Merton Walk (left) to Broad Walk, which passes by Christ Church Meadow to the back of the House. From the Oxford city centre, take High Street and turn left on St. Aldate's going south. The college and Tom Tower are on the left opposite Brewer Street and the Alice in Wonderland Shop or "the Sheep Shop."

Keble College—Where Lewis was stationed after being drafted as a battalion infantryman in the summer of 1917. His address was, "No. 738 Cadet C. S. Lewis, 'E' Company, Keble College, Oxford." Lewis described his quarters at the college as "a carpetless little cell," and thought his training was "very hard and not very interesting." After a leave and an exam, he joined the Somerset Light Infantry near Plymouth, and was sent to France and World War I on 17 November 1917.

Lewis' good friend Austin Farrer (1904–1968) was the Warden at Keble from 1959 till his death. A renowned Anglican theologian, philosopher, and preacher, Farrer published many articles, reviews, books, and sermons during his lifetime, including *A Faith of Our Own*, for which Lewis wrote a glowing introduction to the American edition (1960).

Farrer and Lewis were active in the Oxford Socratic Club, a forum initiated by Miss Stella Aldwinckle of the Oxford pastoral staff for discussions about culture, philosophy, and theology. Often the Socratic Club debates pitted Christians like Farrer and Lewis against atheistic or agnostic philosophers and writers. It was in these debates that Lewis at least partially earned his reputation as a hard-nosed "defender of the faith."

Farrer and his wife Katharine were friends with Joy Lewis, and although the movie *Shadowlands* has Lewis calling Joy the night in Oxford (18 October 1956) when her left femur broke because of advanced cancer, it was really Katharine Farrer who had called, due to a premonition she had that something was wrong with Joy. The Farrers were present at Joy and Jack's first wedding, a civil ceremony, and Farrer was present when Joy died 11 July 1960. He also officiated at her cremation service on 18 July, and conducted Lewis' funeral service at Holy Trinity Church, Headington, on 26 November 1963. Lewis' doctor and fellow Inkling R. E. Havard (1901–1985) was also a graduate of Keble College.

Keble was founded in 1870, as a memorial to Rev. John Keble, one of the leaders of the Oxford Movement (from 1833), a famous religious and political dispute between Anglican and Roman Catholic communions. The college was designed by William Butterfield, one of the great architects of the 19th century. His architecture has been described as a "riot of Victorian Gothic" and a "holy zebra style," with its use of bricks of different colors and sizes to produce patterns.

"To relieve the monotony of his building materials," Butterfield set some windows flush to the walls and set others back; used single, double, and triple windows; varied the skyline in places; and placed a useless chimney stack on the roof of the chapel. It has been said that people "either love Keble or hate it," but its colorful and unusual façade catches the eye. Butterfield's great chapel is almost overwhelming, one of the most beautiful college chapels in England.

Located in a small side chapel is another item of great interest at Keble, Holman Hunt's painting of *The Light of the World*. Completed in 1853, it llustrates Jesus' words from Revelation 3:20, "Behold, I stand at the door, and knock . . ." This famous painting attracts visitors from all over the world.

To reach Keble College, go to St. Giles, just past the city centre and off Banbury Road, between Keble Road and Blackhall Road.

Mansfield College—Where Lewis preached his famous sermon "Transposition" on 28 May 1944. A local newspaper reported that Lewis was so overcome by emotion during the sermon that he had to leave the pulpit for a while. He was assisted by the college principal, and after a hymn was sung, finished the sermon, still with great emotion.

"Transposition," primarily concerned with spirituality, represents some of Lewis' best theological thinking. Many in Lewis' day had protested that Christian spirituality was merely a mirage, a psychological projection—Freudian psychology was the vogue at Oxford when Lewis was there. In this sermon Lewis developed his idea of transposition, which, simply put, means that a person's desire for God has been placed in him or her by God. Lewis believed that God often uses a "lower medium," such as a finite human being, to produce a "higher medium," or a spirit-filled person. Lewis also wrote about this idea in *Miracles* and *Reflections on the Psalms*.

"Transposition" was first published in *Transposition and Other Addresses* (1949, in America as *The Weight of Glory and Other Addresses*), and later in *They Asked for a Paper* (1962) and *Screwtape Proposes a Toast and Other Pieces* (1965).

To reach Mansfield College, the smallest college at Oxford, go from Magdalen College up High Street, turning right on Longwall, then left on Holywell to Mansfield Road on the right. The college is on the left of Mansfield Road, near New Parks Road and the city centre.

Oriel College—Where Lewis sat for exams (5-9 December 1916) to qualify as a scholar at University College. This was his first visit to Oxford. In the 1920s, Lewis sometimes visited Oriel for meetings of the Mermaid Club, founded in 1902 "to promote the reading and study of the Elizabethan and post-Elizabethan drama."

From Magdalen College, Oriel is located on the left of High Street, on the east side of Oriel Square towards the city centre, past University College and just after Magpie Lane. It faces Christ Church's Peckwater Quad and Canterbury Gate. The Hall is usually, though not always, closed to visitors. On the north side of the college is the Senior Common Room, birthplace of the Oxford Movement (see Keble College, p. 22), led by John Keble, John Henry (later Cardinal) Newman, R. H. Froude, and E. B. Pusey—all Fellows of Oriel.

St. Hugh's College—Where Jack and Warren Lewis attended a lecture on Byzantine art given by their friend and fellow

Inkling Gervase Mathew (see Blackfriars, p. 21) on 13 July 1946. Afterwards, Mathew said that Charles Williams, who was not an expert in this research, had given a truer account of Byzantium in his Arthurian poem *Talliessin Through Logres* (1938) than that of his authority Sir Edward Gibbon, author of *The History of the Decline and Fall of the Roman Empire*, who attended Magdalen College in the middle 1700s.

St. Hugh's is located on St. Margaret's Road in North Oxford, near Tolkien's St. Aloysius Church (see p. 40).

University College—Locally called "Univ.," the home of Lewis' undergraduate studies April 1917–1922. (His term was interrupted June 1916–1919 due to military training and service in World War I.) His "school," or course of study, was Honour Moderations (philosophy). After Lewis obtained the B.A. degree in 1922, he returned to the college and taught philosophy in 1924.

Lewis admired the poetry of Shelley (especially *Prometheus Unbound*), who was expelled from Univ. in 1811 for circulating a pamphlet praising atheism. A passage (doorway 3) in the right corner of the Front Quad, built between 1634 and 1677, leads to the Shelley Memorial (1893), which Lewis mentions and praises in *They Stand Together*.

Founded in 1249, Univ. is one of the oldest Oxford colleges; the others are Balliol and Merton. There has been much debate, both heated and amiable, about which is older. The debate has subsided somewhat, as it has been declared that Merton was the first to actually have students and statutes.

Univ. is located on High Street, up from Magdalen College and the Botanic Gardens (left) toward the city centre between Magpie and Logic Lanes. Lewis' rooms at Univ. were in the Front Quad, Number 5, Staircase 12, overlooking the Radcliffe Quad.

Wadham College—Where Lewis' good friends Leo Baker (1898–1986) and Owen Barfield (1898–1998) were students. It was in the lovely Fellows' Garden here that Lewis and Barfield had many of the religious and philosophical discussions that Lewis later called "the Great War." Some of these discussions were no doubt held under a huge, very old copper beech in the garden, which now has a sign at its base proclaiming it to be "the oldest tree in Oxford."

Lewis' friend Sister Penelope Lawson (see Wantage, p. 89) preached in Wadham Chapel on 14 May 1967. Warren Lewis recorded in *Brothers and Friends* that "it is a long time since I've enjoyed a service so much." The Sister's subject at that Evensong service was "the creation of the world interpreted in terms of modern knowledge."

Wadham College, founded in 1610, is located in the city centre on Parks Road, near the New Bodleian Library and the Oxford Music Room.

Pubs, Hotels, Restaurants

Pubs

The Eagle and Child—The meeting place of the "Inklings" from 1939 to 1962. Known locally as the Bird and Baby, the inn was established in 1650 and named after the Earl of Derby, whose family crest pictured an eagle carrying a child. In the Inklings' years, the manager of the pub was Mr. Charles Blagrove, who bore a striking resemblance to C. S. Lewis. Mr. Blagrove allowed the Inklings to use a parlor at the back of the pub (now the center) called "the Rabbit Room" for their meetings and talks (usually on Tuesdays), which have become a part of Christian and literary legend. Interestingly, several detective story writers have mentioned or alluded to the Inklings and the Eagle and Child.

In Edmund Crispin's *Swan Song*, detective and professor Gervase Fen says, "There goes C. S. Lewis; it must be Tuesday." Colin Dexter's Inspector Morse often frequents the Bird, and in *The Secret of Annex Three* his Sergeant Lewis considers the plaque in the Rabbit Room, which reads:

> *C. S. LEWIS, his brother, W. H. Lewis, J. R. R. Tolkien, Charles Williams, and other friends met every Tuesday morning, between the years 1939–1962 in the back room of this their favourite pub. These men, popularly known as the 'Inklings,' met here to drink beer and to discuss, among other things, the books they were writing.*

The Inklings were an informal group; there were no membership qualifications or initiation rites. The group consisted of those invited to the Eagle and Child on Tuesdays or to Lewis' rooms at Magdalen College for Thursday evening discussions. Lewis did ask that manuscripts being written at the time be read by those attending. Nonacademics such as his brother Warren and his doctor R. E. Havard also made contributions to this friendly group.

Most of the Inklings were friends of Lewis, but not all who attended the Tuesday meetings were invited to the Thursday meetings at Magdalen. The Inklings were drawn together because of shared interests in literature, religion, and "general" culture, including politics. The group was not a mutual admiration society when it came to the works that were read. Praise flowed freely for good work, but bad or even "average" work was often censored in very frank terms.

In addition to Lewis and Warren, other men who were involved in the Inklings from the beginning, around 1933 (before the Tuesday meetings at the Eagle and Child) to the end were: Owen Barfield of Wadham College, who was Lewis' lawyer and attended infrequently; Lord David Cecil of Wadham College and Goldsmith's Professor of English Literature for the University of Oxford; "Hugo" Dyson, a Fellow of Merton College; and J. R. R. Tolkien, a founder and regular member.

Those who attended Inklings meetings in the early period but who did not attend later were: Nevill Coghill, a Fellow and Tutor of Exeter College and Merton professor of English Language; Adam Fox, a Fellow of Magdalen College and Professor of Poetry; R. E. Havard, Lewis and Tolkien's personal physician; and Charles L. Wrenn, Tolkien's successor as Rawlinson and Bosworth professor of Anglo-Saxon.

Those who attended meetings starting in the 1940s were: Charles W. S. Williams, Editor of Oxford University Press; J. A. W. Bennett, a pupil of Lewis and Tutor at Magdalen who succeeded Lewis at Cambridge; Roy Campbell, a South African poet and professional bullfighter; Jim Dundas-Grant, Commander of Oxford University Naval Division; Alan Bede Griffiths, a pupil of Lewis and a public orator; Colin Hardie, Classics Tutor and Fellow of Balliol; Gervase Mathew, University Lecturer in Byzantine Studies; R. B. McCallum, Master of Pembroke College; George Sayer, a pupil of Lewis and his later biographer; Tom Stevens, a Fellow at Magdalen College; Christopher Tolkien, the youngest son of J. R. R. Tolkien and a Fellow at New College; and John Wain, a pupil of Lewis, Professor of Poetry, and later a successful novelist.

The Eagle and Child is located near the city centre, on Woodstock Road (49 St. Giles), a few blocks from the Ashmolean Museum, Blackfriars, and Pusey House.

The Checquers—Often visited by Jack and Warren Lewis, and mentioned in *Brothers and Friends*. It was a private house from 1260 to 1434, and afterwards was used by a moneylender till about 1460. Established as a tavern in 1500, some of the original oak paneling, a stone fireplace, and carved stonework still remain.

For the first-time visitor to Oxford, the Checquers is fairly hard to find. Located at 131a High Street, it can be reached by going down an alleyway right of the High going east towards Magdalen Bridge.

The King's Arms—A favorite of Jack and Warren Lewis' friend Charles Williams. In *Brothers and Friends*, Warren Lewis reported that when he first heard the news of Williams' death on 15 May 1945, he felt "dazed and restless" and went to the King's Arms to get a drink. Warren lamented after Williams' death, "The Inklings can never be the same again." After World War II, King's was used for meetings of the Inklings when the Eagle and Child was closed for a while due to a beer shortage.

Established in 1609, the King's Arms is one of Oxford's most famous pubs. Formerly a coaching inn, it was also an informal theatre. The first Oxford production of *Hamlet* was performed here, and it has been used several times for the popular *Inspector Morse* TV series.

The King's Arms is located downtown facing Broad Street on the corner of Parks Road and Holywell Road, near Blackwell's, the Sheldonian Theatre, and the Clarendon Building.

The Lamb and Flag—Popular with Lewis and his friends, and used for Inklings meetings in 1962 when the Eagle and Child was renovated and provided less privacy for meetings. After Lewis' death in 1963, a few Inklings meetings were held at the Lamb, but without Lewis, they were soon abandoned.

Located at 12 St. Giles, directly across from the Eagle and Child in downtown Oxford, the Lamb and Flag dates from 1695. Parts of the original building remain. Originally owned by Godstow Abbey on the outskirts of Oxford, its name was derived from the symbol of John the Baptist.

The Six Bells—An establishment Lewis visited often and that is mentioned and pictured in *C. S. Lewis: Images of His World*. This friendly old neighborhood "locals" pub is located at 8 Beaumont Road, Headington. It is almost directly next (east) to Lewis' "home" church, Holy Trinity, and is within easy walking distance of the Kilns, Lewis' Oxford home from 1930 until his death.

The White Horse—Used for Inklings meetings toward the end of World War II due to the closing of the Eagle and Child for a time. This small 18th-century pub stands on 52 Broad Street between Blackwell's bookstore and the entrance to Balliol College. Like the King's Arms, it is rumored that the White Horse was Inspector Morse's favorite watering hole.

Hotels

The Eastgate Hotel—Frequented by Lewis and his friends (J. R. R. Tolkien came here often, especially in his later years when he lived in retirement on Merton Street) and also the site of Jack and Joy's first meeting after corresponding for 2 years. Joy's marriage to Bill Gresham was disintegrating due in part to his violent nature, and she was scared and thinking about divorce. She had been a Christian for several years, and after much thought decided to travel to England and meet Lewis, whose works had been influential to her growing faith.

Joy had arranged to stay in London with a "pen pal" named Phyllis Williams. She wrote to Lewis in early September 1952, inviting him to lunch at the Eastgate. On

Wednesday, 24 September 1952, the two women traveled to Oxford to see Lewis and met him in the dining room of the hotel. Lewis was captivated immediately by Joy. He quickly invited her and Phyllis to have lunch with him and his brother Warren at his rooms at Magdalen. Warren backed out of the luncheon at the last minute, and Lewis invited his friend and former student George Sayer to take his place. Sayer was impressed with Joy as well. He especially admired her taste in clothes and makeup and her quick wit.

The Eastgate was also the location of the first meeting in the mid-1950s between Lewis and science-fiction writer Arthur C. Clarke. The meeting was probably arranged by Joy Gresham, who had given Lewis a copy of Clarke's *Childhood's End* (1954). Lewis was "bowled over" by the book. Later Clarke sent him a collection of short stories called *Expedition to Earth* (1954).

For years Clarke had wanted to meet Lewis and discuss the differences the two men had about science fiction societies and interplanetary exploration. In *Perelandra* (1943), Lewis had mentioned "the little rocket societies that take humankind's crimes and sin to other planets," and in other writings seemed to be cynical about scientists in general. After this meeting, although neither man persuaded the other, Lewis told Clarke (no doubt with a gleam in his eye), "I'm sure you're very wicked people—but how dull it would be if everyone was good."

Another first meeting at the Eastgate was that of Joy Lewis and Ruth Pitter (see p. 87) on 1 February 1954. Joy did not make a favorable impression on Ruth. They did correspond a few times, but Ruth never visited the Kilns while Joy was living there.

The Eastgate Hotel is situated at 73 High Street and occupies the site of an inn known as the Crosse Sword, which dates from 1605. In 1840, the Flying Horse Inn occupied the site, and in 1899 was replaced by the Eastgate. It is located just up and across the street from Lewis' Magdalen College, on the corner of Merton Street past Rose Lane.

The Mitre—Frequented by Lewis and his friends during his time at Oxford. On 29 January 1940, Lewis, Tolkien, and Charles Williams celebrated at the Mitre after Williams' first lecture at Oxford, at the University Divinity School. In early 1945, Lewis' friend and fellow Inkling Father Gervase Mathew arranged for Lewis to meet T. S. Eliot for the first time at the Mitre, along with Charles Williams. This famous meeting was an uneasy one, due to the fact that Lewis had been critical of Eliot's poetry. Both men were wary of each other. Although Eliot did not ease the tension by remarking that Lewis "looked older than his photographs," the two later became friends when working on a revision of *The Book of Common Prayer.*

The Mitre is a very old inn, situated on the corner of High and Turl Streets. Dating from about 1300, it is one of only 3 ancient Oxford inns that have survived into the 20th century. The name "mitre" was probably adapted from the herald crest of Lincoln College, the owner of the inn since the 15th century. The crest pictures a mitre (hat or headdress worn by bishops and abbots) above the see (diocese) of Lincoln. Since 1967, the Mitre's landlords have been the Berni Inns, and it has been used solely as a restaurant, with the upper rooms reserved for members of Lincoln. The Mitre is an unusual inn architecturally. After Arthur C. Clarke stayed here in the 1950s, he described it as a "wonderful, non-Euclidean building with no right angles in it, no two rooms the same."

The Randolph Hotel—A site Lewis and his friends often passed while on walks, and where they occasionally visited and entertained guests. Built in 1863, this "4-star" hotel, Oxford's finest, is located on Beaumont Street, across from the Ashmolean Museum in downtown Oxford. Its Spires Restaurant and Lancaster Room both contain paintings by Sir Osbert Lancaster, commissioned to illustrate Max Beerbohm's classic satire on Oxford life, *Zuleika Dobson.* The writer Henry James often stayed at the Randolph and once wrote that it was ideally situated for visiting and "strolling from college to college."

Studley Priory Hotel—A favorite meeting place of Joy and Jack Lewis and the Inklings. Lewis loved to eat Sunday lunch at Studley and often went there with some of the Inklings and other friends. On 15 April 1958, Lewis wrote to his friend Mary Willis Shelbourne in America (*Letters to an American Lady*) and mentioned that he and his wife Joy had shared "what we never had before, a honeymoon!" This delayed honeymoon, one of at least 2 they took in England and Ireland (see Crawfordsburn, p. 4), was taken at the Studley Priory, a favorite place of the Lewis' before and after their honeymoon.

Douglas Gresham wrote in *Lenten Lands* that his mother met and became friends with the journalist Jean Wakeman at Studley, probably in the late 1950s. Miss Wakeman became a great encouragement to Joy during her illness and often took her for trips around the country when Jack and her boys were away at school.

In the 12th century, the Priory was a Benedictine nunnery. After the monasteries were abolished under Henry VIII, the Priory was purchased by the Croke family, who held it for 335 years. A chapel was added in 1639, and another wing in 1666, but otherwise the exterior of Studley has stayed much the same since Elizabethan times.

To reach Studley Priory, located about 7 miles from the city centre, travel to the end of Banbury Road (north). At the roundabout take the third exit (towards London) and travel for about 3½ miles. At the next roundabout take the first exit posted as "Horton-Cum-Studley." Proceed along Baywater Road until you reach the staggered crossroads. Follow signs to Horton-Cum-Studley for 2½ miles. Continue straight on the road into the village. The hotel is situated on the top of the hill on the right.

Restaurants

The Trout—A favorite place of Lewis and his friends, where they would often come in the summertime and sit outdoors and enjoy the scenery. There are pictures of the inn in *Through Joy and Beyond* and *C. S. Lewis: Images of His World*, and pictures of Inklings Jim Dundas-Grant, Colin Hardie, Dr. R. E. Havard, and Lewis sitting at the Trout in *Through Joy and Beyond* and *The Inklings*.

Originally a fisherman's home in the 16th century, this inn and restaurant is one of Oxford's most popular and is known by generations of students, townspeople, and visitors to the city. Known for its wandering peacocks and view across Port Meadow to the "dreaming spires," the Trout is an idyllic and beautiful setting. Its many literary and historical associations lend to its charm. It was mentioned in

Matthew Arnold's poem "The Scholar Gypsy," and is where the novelist Evelyn Waugh often stopped for breakfast. On a lazy afternoon in 1862, Professor Charles Ludwig Dodgson ("Lewis Carroll") and Alice Liddell and her two sisters rowed down the Isis (Thames River) as far as the Trout. It was here in Carroll's fertile imagination that Alice fell down a rabbit hole, and later her story was immortalized in *Alice's Adventures in Wonderland*.

The Trout is located on Godstow Road, Wolvercote (a suburb of Oxford), and can be reached by walking or cycling along the Isis for the length of Port Meadow, past Godstow Lock and the 12th-century nunnery, or by car through Wolvercote Village from the top of Woodstock Road.

C. S. Lewis' Homes

Between 1916 and 1930, Lewis lived in 8 homes in the Oxford area before he moved into the Kilns, the home most often associated with him. In most of these residences he lived with his "adopted family," the Moores. Later, after Warren Lewis' return from military duty, he lived with them in the Kilns.

In his diary *All My Road Before Me*, Lewis listed and commented negatively on some of these homes. It is interesting that 2 of the homes he mentioned, "Mrs. Adam's, Invermore," and "Lindon Cottage on the other side of Headington," cannot be located today. Mr. Peter Cousin, a taxi driver in Oxford who specializes in Lewis tours and is treasurer of the Oxford C. S. Lewis Society, has scoured Headington unsuccessfully to find them, and other reliable sources in Oxford have had a similar lack of success.

1 Mansfield Road—In *Surprised By Joy*, Lewis told that when he first came to Oxford in 1916, he lived in a house that was "the first on the right as you turn into Mansfield Road out of Holywell." According to all accounts, the house looks almost exactly the same today as it did in Lewis' time.

Anstey Villas, 28 Warneford Road—To locate this residence, travel out Cowley Road (east) and turn left on either Divinity Road, Bartlemas Road, or Southfield Road; all of these will turn into Warneford Road. The Moores came here first in January 1919, then moved to Windmill Road, and returned here in the summer of 1922.

Hillview, 76 Windmill Road—In August 1919, the Moores moved to Hillview, the home of Mr. and Mrs. Albert Morris. Lewis described the house as a flat where "we had 2 rooms and I slept on a sofa." Windmill Road is located in Headington, near the main business district and Old High Street, to the right off Headington Road.

58 Windmill Road—The Moores and Lewis' next move was early in February 1920 to this house a few blocks down the street from Hillview. The owner is mentioned in *They Stand Together* as Mrs. John Jeffrey, "a butcher by occupation." It was here that Lewis first read Wordsworth's *The Prelude*, one of the most influential books in his life, and one he reread many times.

Courtfield Cottage, 131 Osler Road, Headington—Osler Road is located just off Headington Road (left), past Sandfield Road where Tolkien lived and before Windmill Road.

Hillsboro House, 14 Holyoake Road—Lewis and the Moores lived here from 30 April 1923 until the time they moved to the Kilns in October 1930. The residence now houses the Oxford Chiropractic Clinic.

The Kilns, Headington—The Kilns was built in 1922 on 9 acres. Originally the property had a garden, tennis court, large pond, greenhouse, and the remains of a brick kilns. In the late 1800s, the property was used for the quarrying of clay used for making bricks, and the pond in the present nature reserve was the original pit from which the clay was dug. Lewis, his brother Warren, and Mrs. Moore bought the Kilns for £3,300, and they, along with Mrs. Moore's daughter Maureen, moved into the house on 10 October 1930. The gardener Fred Paxford (the possible model for Puddleglum the Marshwiggle in *The Silver Chair*) came to the Kilns in late 1930 and stayed till Lewis' death in 1963. Through the years the household also employed maids, with Mrs. Molly Miller coming as permanent housemaid in 1952.

The Kilns, Headington, Oxford

Picture of C. S. Lewis inside the Kilns

The Kilns originally had 4 bedrooms, a kitchen, 2 reception rooms, a pantry, and a small maid's bedroom; 2 additional rooms were added in 1932. The Lewis brothers and Mrs. Moore made many improvements to the property, including building new fences and adding walking paths. Lewis loved to walk in the woods on the property, especially during the spring and fall. Although not a gardener, he loved to putter around the garden and help Mrs. Moore the best he could.

Garden at the Kilns, Headington, Oxford

Joy Gresham and her sons moved into the Kilns in early 1958, after her diagnosis of cancer. As the movie *Shadowlands* portrays, she made many improvements to the house, including painting, redecorating, crocheting rugs, and buying new china. The "old bachelor" Lewis brothers were notoriously bad housekeepers, and when Joy moved in, she found holes in the walls and floors, carpets in rags, and general disarray. Lewis lived in the Kilns until his death in 1963. After Jack's death, Warren moved away from the Kilns for about 3 years, then returned to live in the home until his own death in April 1973.

In the late 1960s, some of the property to the east of the house was sold for the purpose of development. In 1969, several acres of woodlands and the pond were sold to an Oxfordshire Trust and made into the "Henry Stephen/ C. S. Lewis Nature Reserve," Mr. Stephen being the gentleman who lived in the house next to the Kilns. In 1973, the house was sold to the Thirsk family by Maureen Moore, who inherited it after the death of Warnie Lewis. Many repairs and additions were made, including the installation of central heating, new plumbing, and a new garage. The house was acquired in 1984 by a group of investors who later donated it to the organization that became the C. S. Lewis Foundation of Redlands, California. Since 1993, restoration has begun on the house.

To locate the Kilns, go out to the end of Headington Road (east), and then through the roundabout (right) across the Eastern Bypass (A4142) to Green Road. Follow Green a few blocks till it becomes Kiln Lane. Look for Lewis Close on the right, the first street past Netherwoods Road. The Kilns is at the end of the Close on the right. Remember, this is a neighborhood, and although the residents are quite used to people coming to look at the Kilns, visitors should exercise courtesy and discretion in taking photos and walking around the property.

Other Homes of Interest

4 Broad Street—Home of the famed Irish poet W. B. Yeats, whom Lewis visited at least twice. He described his impressions of Yeats in detail in a letter to his brother Warren on 13 March 1921 (*Letters of C. S. Lewis*, revised and enlarged edition, 1993). Lewis modeled the magician in his narrative poem *Dymer* (1926) after Yeats, and may have also modeled his Merlin the Magician in *That Hideous Strength* after him.

10 Old High Street, Headington—The residence to which Joy Gresham moved from London, in August 1955, with her sons Douglas and David and their cat Sambo. Located in Oxford, about a mile from the Kilns, the house was a duplex and had room for a garden out back, in which Joy planted flowers, herbs, and fruit. It also had a small kitchen, a dining room, a parlor, a bathroom, and 3 bedrooms. Lewis found the house for the Gresham family, encouraged them to move, and paid their rent, which was much higher than at their Belsize Park residence in London (see Avoca House Hotel, p. 91).

To locate Joy's home, go out Headington Road a few miles into the Headington business district. Old High is the first street past Stephen Road (left). The house is the first one on the left.

10 Old High Street, Headington, Oxford.

Places Special to Lewis' Friends

J. R. R. Tolkien

J. R. R. Tolkien (1892–1973) was a great friend of C. S. Lewis, a member of the Inklings, and the world-famous author of the fantasy classics *The Hobbit, The Lord of the Rings* trilogy, and *The Silmarillion*. He first met Lewis in May 1926, and the two remained friends for the rest of their lives. Tolkien was instrumental in Lewis' conversion to Christianity and helped his friend gain an important appointment to a professorship at Cambridge.

Tolkien came to Oxford in 1911 as an undergraduate at Exeter College, and as his biographer Humphrey Carpenter wrote (*Tolkien: A Biography*, 1977), "already as the car bowled into Oxford he had decided that he would be happy there." Tolkien lived in Oxford for most of his remaining life. Following is a listing of his places.

Exeter College—Tolkien had received a scholarship at Exeter to read "Greats" (classics), and his studies began in the Michaelmas term of 1911. His rooms were in what is now Blackwell's Art and Poster Shop in downtown Oxford, overlooking Turl Street near Exeter.

50 St. John's Street—Tolkien's residence after serving in World War I. It is located near his old digs at Exeter. Tolkien worked for the New English Dictionary, housed in the old Ashmolean Building (now the Museum of the History of Science and the first purpose-built museum in England) on nearby Broad Street. He later moved to #1 Alfred Street, now called Pusey (#1 no longer exists).

Pembroke College—Where Tolkien served as the Rawlinson and Bosworth Professor of Anglo-Saxon. Pembroke is located in St. Aldate's on Brewer Street. From 1920 to 1925, he was a professor in the English Department at Leeds University.

22 Northmoor Road—The residence of Tolkien while at Pembroke, 1926–1929. Until the late 19th century, most Oxford professors and clergy lived at or near their colleges and were not permitted to marry while holding a teaching position. After the turn of the century, reform changed the look of the city, especially North Oxford, with new schools, churches, shops, and residences built to serve the needs of professors and their families. By the 1920s, much of the available property in fashionable North Oxford was occupied, but Tolkien and wife Edith found a new house here.

Northmoor Road is to the right (going north) and parallel to Banbury Road, and intersects Belbroughton Road on the north and Linton Road on the south. It is near the famed Dragon School for boys, which was established in 1877 to provide secondary school education for the sons of University residents and professors. Some of the school's more notable graduates include the historical novelist Naomi Mitchison (girls were admitted in 1910), whose work C. S. Lewis admired; the noted scientist J. B. S. Haldane, with whom Lewis often disagreed over matters of science and faith; and Sir John Betjeman, Poet Laureate and former student of Lewis.

20 Northmoor Road—The residence of the Tolkiens from 1930 to 1947. Located one door down from their previous residence, it had been vacated by Basil Blackwell, a bookseller and publisher. Its spaciousness appealed to the growing family. By this time, the family included children John (born 1916), Michael (born 1920), Christopher (born 1924), and Priscilla (born 1929).

Church of St. Aloysius, 25 Woodstock Road—The church where Tolkien usually worshiped. Founded by the Jesuits in 1870, with help from donations by John Henry Newman and other notables, the church was dedicated in 1875. St. Aloysius is noted for its Victorian-Gothic style architecture, beautifully carved reliefs of the church fathers, and murals. A font set between the arches that separate the narthex from the nave is a memorial to the acclaimed poet Gerard Manley Hopkins, also a priest at the church from 1878 to 1879. Hopkins' poem "God's Grandeur" was much admired by Lewis.

St. Aloysius is located up Woodstock Road in North Oxford and sits on the corner of Woodstock and St. Margaret's Road.

Church of St. Anthony of Padua, 115 Headley Way—Often visited by Tolkien, the church's generous benefactor. When he died in 1973, his requiem mass was held here. St. Anthony was the saint who retrieved lost objects, and a friend of St. Francis. He may have been chosen as patron of this church as a tribute to the Franciscan Order, who served previously in this neighborhood.

To locate St. Anthony's, go up Headington Road past Headington School (left) and turn left on Headley. St. Anthony is a yellow brick church with a green roof situated on the right past Staunton Road (right) near Eden Drive.

Church of St. Gregory and St. Augustine, 322 Woodstock Road—Often visited by Tolkien. Located on Woodstock Road in North Oxford, St. Gregory's was built on land once owned by the Duke of Marlborough. His oldest son John was ordained into the Roman Catholic priesthood here in February 1946. Noted for its unspoiled, rustic charm, the church was established in the early 1900s to provide Catholics who lived to the north of Oxford a convenient place of worship, St. Aloysius being at the southern end of Woodstock Road.

Merton College—Where Tolkien served as Professor of English Language and Literature from 1945 until his retirement in 1959. He found the college "agreeably informal" after Pembroke. Tolkien and his wife Edith celebrated their golden wedding anniversary at Merton, and an event held in their honor was a performance of Donald Swann's song-cycle, *The Road Goes Ever On*. The singer was a man named William Elven, whose name Tolkien later said "was a name of good omen!"

Merton was founded in 1264 and claims to be the oldest college at Oxford, although this is sometimes debated, especially by those who favor University College. Some of its more famous graduates include John Wyclif, Max Beerbohm, Lord Randolph Churchill, and T. S. Eliot.

Merton is famous for its interesting and very old and medieval buildings, especially the chapel, which has an impressive bell tower. Merton's small and oddly named college quadrangle, Mob Quad, has been called "the oldest quadrangle in the oldest college in the oldest university in the world." The quad is the home of Merton's famous Old Library, the oldest library in regular use in Europe, established between 1337 and 1338. It is a treasure house of ancient manuscripts; medieval astrological instruments, including an astrolabe said to have been used by Chaucer; stained glass; and a 13th-century oak chest.

To reach Merton, turn right (east) out of University College on High Street and right into Logic Lane. This will lead to cobbled Merton Street, one of the prettiest and least explored streets in Oxford. In front of you will be the Merton bell tower, not as tall as the one at Magdalen but with a similar stunning effect.

3 Manor Road—A house owned by Merton College, and the residence of Tolkien from 1947 to 1950. The large family house on Northmoor Road had to be given up when the household was reduced to Tolkien, Edith, and Priscilla, the older boys having grown up and moved away.

To reach Manor Road, turn right (west) out of Magdalen College up High Street to Longwall on the right. Follow Longwall past the St. Cross church (right), and the road becomes Manor, which leads further to St. Catherine's College.

99 Holywell Street—A home owned by Merton College, and the residence of Tolkien from 1950 to 1953. This old house was admired by the Tolkiens for its "character" and large number of rooms. Tolkien, Edith, and Priscilla moved here from Manor Road (only a few hundred yards away from Parks Road) in the early spring of 1950. After the cramped confines in Manor Road, they enjoyed this 17th-century house with its small garden and high medieval wall dividing it from the New College gardens. The semidetached house had a small step up from the street and was angled back, prompting son Christopher to remark that it "looked like someone leaning back after a good dinner."

76 Sandfield Road, Headington—The home of the Tolkiens from 1953 to 1968. In the early 1950s, the city of Oxford had perhaps its greatest growth of new residents and tourists. Due to increasing traffic and noise, the Tolkien family decided to move to this smaller, quieter home in Headington. They soon learned to enjoy the pleasant garden and quiet surroundings.

To reach Sandfield Road, go east on Headington Road, past Headington Hill Park, Pullens Lane, and Headington School; then turn left on Sandfield. A plaque on the front of the house (left side of street) records the times the Tolkien family lived here.

21 Merton Street—Tolkien's residence in Oxford after his wife's death in March 1972 (see Bournemouth, p. 82). He lived at this flat (now a condominium) next to the Eastgate Hotel, which was given to him expense-free by Merton College. The College also made him a resident honorary Fellow and offered him the services of a caretaker named Mr. Carr, who lived in the basement with his wife. The Carrs were very kind to Tolkien and provided him with breakfast and lunch or dinner if he did not feel well or did not wish to dine at Merton.

The *Pinas Nigra* tree and "the two trees"—Tolkien's favorite tree (the *Pinas Nigra*) and trees planted in his honor. The *Pinas Nigra* is in the Botanic Garden, opposite Magdalen College off High Street. A famous photo of Tolkien, the last one taken of him (on 9 August 1973) standing next to the tree, is in Humphrey Carpenter's *Tolkien: A Biography*. In 1992, in honor of Tolkien, the Tolkien Society planted 2 trees, a silver-leafed maple and a *False Acacia*, in the University Parks and placed a memorial bench there. These are located in the north centre of the city, to the right of Parks Road and to the north of the University and Pitt Rivers museums. Part of this area is a nature reserve (where the trees and bench are), part of it forms the grounds of the Oxford Cricket Club, and the rest is occupied by science facilities and laboratories. Tolkien's trees stand at the left of the gardens facing from Magdalen College, near the back wall.

Wolvercote Cemetery, North Oxford—Where Tolkien was buried following his death at Bournemouth, Dorset, on Sunday morning, 2 September 1973, as a result of complications from an acute gastric bleeding ulcer and chest infection. The funeral service was held at St. Anthony of Padua church, and he was buried at this cemetery on the outskirts of Oxford, where a section is reserved for Roman Catholics. The gravestone reads:

> *Edith Mary Tolkien, Luthien, 1889–1971, John Ronald*
> *Reuel Tolkien, Beren, 1892–1973*

This epitaph refers to Tolkien's story of the love between Beren, a mortal man, and Luthien, an elf maiden in *The Silmarillion.*

To reach the cemetery, go up Headington Road, past Headley Way (left), and Sandfield Road. Turn left on Osler Road, pass Ivy lane (left), and bear left on Dunstan Road. The cemetery is just past Ethelred Court on the left on Dunstan.

Charles Williams

Charles W. S. Williams (1886–1945) was a valued friend of C. S. Lewis, a member of the Inklings, and the author of "supernatural thrillers" such as *War in Heaven* (1930), *The Place of the Lion* (1931), and *Descent into Hell* (1937). The former has one of the greatest opening lines in any novel: "The telephone bell was ringing wildly, but without result, since there was no one in the room but the corpse." Williams was also an editor at Oxford University Press and a prolific writer of plays, poetry, biographies, literary criticism, and church history. Among his several religious works are: *He Came Down From Heaven* (1938) and *The Forgiveness of Sins* (1942).

Williams influenced many notable scholars including C. S. Lewis, W. H. Auden, Dorothy L. Sayers, and T. S. Eliot. Williams was especially a profound influence on Lewis, as one can see in Lewis' works *That Hideous Strength* and *The Four Loves*.

Lewis and Williams first became acquainted when they exchanged mutual "fan letters" almost at the same time in 1936. Lewis thought *The Place of the Lion* was one of the best novels he had ever read, and Williams was an admirer of *The Allegory of Love*. Williams and Lewis most likely met for the first time in 1938 in London, and became good friends in 1940 when the Press moved to Oxford to escape Hitler's blitz. (The German leader had vowed to make Oxford his capital when Europe was captured, thus making Oxford a safe haven.)

Although Williams lived in Oxford for only 5 years, his influence on the city and University has been profound. The best short introduction to him, both as a person and as a writer, is Lewis' preface in *Essays Presented to Charles Williams* (1947). The following is a listing of some of Williams' places in Oxford.

9 South Parks Road—The large Victorian residence of Professor H. N. Spalding, with whom Williams lived when he moved with the Press to Oxford in September 1939. Williams had come to know the Spalding family when one of his plays had been produced in Oxford earlier by daughter Ruth Spalding, who worked for an Oxford drama society (see p. 45). The Spalding house, now demolished, was located in the city centre, near Broad Street and the Sheldonian Theatre. The site is now occupied by part of the complex housing the Department of Zoology of the University of Oxford.

Southfield House, Hilltop Road, Cowley—Location of the Press' temporary offices in Oxford, a little more than a mile from the city centre. Cowley is an old suburb of Oxford, and Southfield House stood on a rise between Cowley and Headington Roads near the Magdalen Arms pub, which faces Iffley Road.

The University Church of St. Mary the Virgin, High Street (see p. 58)—The site of the production, in June 1939, of Williams' nativity play *The Seed of Adam*. His friend Ruth Spalding was the producer. The play was written about 1936 at the request of the Chelmsford (London) Diocesan Religious Drama Guild for performance in that diocese. Miss Spalding subsequently produced 3 performances for her new Oxford Drama branch of the Pilgrim Players, initially formed at Canterbury.

The play has no commentator, only actors and 2 choruses, and is characterized by its splendid use of language, perhaps the best in all of Williams' plays. *The Seed of Adam* is rich in dramatic symbolism, and is a powerful statement of Williams' love for God, as the last lines by Joseph and the chorus make clear: "Blessed be he whose love is the knowledge of good and its motion the willing of good: blessed be he. Adore, adore: blessed for evermore be the Lord God Sabbaoth: blessed be he." The play was published in 1948 as *The Seed of Adam and Other Plays*, with an excellent introduction by Anne Ridler. The other plays in the collection are *The Death of Good Fortune*, the widely performed *The House by the Stable*, and *Grab and Grace*.

Lady Margaret Hall; The Old Library, St. Mary's Church; Pusey House; St. Hilda's College; The Taylor Institution ("Taylorian"); the University Divinity School—Places where Williams lectured while living in Oxford. Although he was not on the faculty and did not have an earned degree, Williams was allowed to guest lecture due primarily to the influence of Lewis.

In January and February 1940, Williams lectured on Milton at the Divinity School. These lectures went so well and were so popular with undergraduates that opportunities for other lectures started to open. He lectured and tutored regularly at St. Hilda's, a few blocks southeast of Magdalen College off Cowley Plain. Until 1943, he gave 16 lectures a year on Wordsworth and Shakespeare at the Taylorian, next to the Ashmolean Museum on St. Giles. Williams also gave lectures on English literature and Shakespeare at Lady Margaret Hall in St. Giles near Norham Road.

Williams' series on Christian literature at Pusey House was especially well received. Pusey House is a Catholic private hall, founded in 1884 as a memorial to Dr. E. B. Pusey, who for 50 years was Professor of Hebrew and Canon of Christ Church. Located in St. Giles near the Eagle and Child, next to Blackfriars, today the hall is the home of the Oxford C. S. Lewis Society.

Williams also lectured on religion and drama at the Old Library (now used as a parish meeting room) of St. Mary's University Church. His lectures were so successful that the prestigious Oxford Danté Society wanted him as a member, and his friends—especially Lewis—wanted him on the English faculty. Both of these required a University degree, so on 18 February 1943, Williams was awarded an honorary Master of Arts.

The Radcliffe Hospital (now Infirmary)—The hospital where Williams died. In mid-morning of Tuesday, 15 May 1945, Warren Lewis received a message that Williams had died. Never strong physically, Charles was often tired and overworked and had been admitted to the Radcliffe after suffering severe stomach pain. He was operated on for a recurrence of the gastric trouble he had had 11 years previously, but never regained consciousness. His sudden death was like a hammer blow to Lewis and the Inklings, for Williams was admired and loved by almost everyone who knew him.

For a week or so after Williams' death, Lewis had a strong sense of his presence, and said later that he believed in life after death even more than before. He wrote to a friend that Williams' death "has made my faith stronger than it was a week ago," and made the point again in the preface for *Essays Presented to Charles Williams*.

The Infirmary is located on Woodstock Road, on the left a few blocks north of the Eagle and Child and near Somerville College. Opened in 1770, the Infirmary is perhaps most recognized as the hospital where the first intravenous injection of penicillin was administered on 27 January 1941. C. S. Lewis' wife Joy also died here on 14 July 1960, after a long and courageous battle with cancer.

Sheldon and Jean Vanauken

Sheldon ("Van") and Jean ("Davy") Vanauken were young Virginians who were close friends of Lewis in the early 1950s while Sheldon was a student at Jesus College. In 1977, Sheldon wrote his autobiography *A Severe Mercy*, which tells the story of his marriage to Davy, their conversions to Christianity while at Oxford, and her untimely death in 1955. Still available in paperback, the book won many awards and is now considered a classic.

A significant part of *A Severe Mercy* tells of the Vanaukens' friendship with Lewis and his spiritual impact on their lives and the part he played as mentor after Davy's death. The book is the single longest account available of the known influence of Lewis on the lives of specific persons, and sheds much light on Lewis as a Christian witness. It contains 18 letters from Lewis to the Vanaukens, many of which show Lewis at his best as a wise and caring friend.

Another wonderful aspect of the book is the picture it evokes of Oxford in the 1950s, "that sweet city with her dreaming spires," an idyllic place of bells and wonderful old churches and lunches at pubs, and most of all, a time of good talk and good learning about faith. Many of the favorite places of the Vanaukens were also Lewis' places. A listing of these follows.

St. Ebbe's Church, Pennyfarthing Place—A church that Van and Davy visited often. Even though they visited several churches in Oxford, including St. Mary's University Church and St. Mary Magdalen, the "ancient Norman Church of St. Ebbe's, evangelical and Church of England" was their favorite. They particularly enjoyed knowing the rector, M. A. P. Wood, who Van called "a great preacher and wise counselor." They met with him several times for lunch at the Rectory in Paradise Square near the church to the west. Now the office of a government agency, it was built in 1855.

The church at St. Ebbe's stands now on the site of a church dedicated in 1005 to Ebbe, a 7th-century saint. Roger Bacon (died 1294) is buried in the parish grounds. St. Ebbe's is much the same today as when the Vanaukens attended, with the addition of a new parish center and bookshop. It is located in the city centre, near Pembroke Street and the Westgate Shopping Center.

Magdalen College and the Eastgate Hotel—A favorite meeting spot for Lewis and Van. Van met several times with Lewis in his rooms at Magdalen. On the very first occasion he found Jack "as simple and unaffected as a man could be" and "the most friendly, the most genial of companions." They often strolled around Addison's Walk and the college grounds talking. In fact, Van wrote that Lewis "walked me off my legs." He heard Lewis lecture often at various schools in the University and at the Socratic Club debates, where "Lewis was in his element."

Lewis and Van's usual meeting place was at the Eastgate for lunch, where Lewis upon entering "would immediately boom out: 'Any pies today?' " Once when Lewis forgot a lunch at the hotel with Van, he sent a note the next day apologizing and asking forgiveness. After their last meeting at the Eastgate, when Lewis had said his farewells and had crossed High Street to the Magdalen side, he looked back at Van with a big grin and roared across the noise of the traffic, "Besides, Christians *never* say goodbye!"

The Perch, Binsey—A favorite of the Vanukens and their friends, including Lewis. This 17th-century "thatched village" inn is noteworthy as being one of the first places in Oxford where Lewis Carroll gave readings of *Alice in Wonderland*. Until it was severely damaged by fire in 1977, it contained oak beams, flagged floors, and stone fireplaces.

The Church of St. Margaret at Binsey—Another favorite place of Van and Davy's. Here they would throw a penny into the wishing well to make their wishes come true. The well water has long been said to be beneficial to those with eye problems. The term "treacle well" came from these traditional legends, and they so caught the imagination of Lewis Carroll that he introduced the term into the conversation at the Mad Hatter's tea party in his Alice stories. The word treacle is derived from the Latin *theriaca* ("antidote").

The Studio, Pusey Lane—A "tiny mews flat" (now demolished) in downtown Oxford where Van and Davy once lived. Here they could hear "all the bells of Oxford," and share with friends, including Lewis, who visited several times. In *A Severe Mercy*, Van called the Studio "inconvenient, damp, smoky, and very dear to us and many."

The Trout, Godstow—The Vanaukens' "favorite place in all the university." Here they had lunch, drank brown ale on the terrace, and fed the swans. Afterwards they would walk back to town along the Isis and watch the college boat races. This beautiful pub and restaurant was also much favored by Lewis (see p. 32).

Other Places of Interest

The Ashmolean Museum—A famous museum on Beaumont Street in downtown Oxford well known to Lewis and his friends. It houses an impressive collection of archaeological and artistic treasures including Greek, Egyptian, and Oriental antiquities and a broad range of English and European paintings from the Renaissance to the present day. Its print room contains a most impressive selection of drawings by Raphael and Michelangelo. The Medieval Room holds the famous "Alfred Jewel," found in 1693 in Somerset, where King Alfred spent the winter of 878 in hiding.

The museum's other rich and varied collections include medieval musical instruments, medieval and Renaissance ceramics and porcelain, old and rare coins, and many more individual items, such as Powhattan's mantle, Guy Fawkes' lantern, and Cromwell's death-mask. The Ashmolean is the oldest museum in the British Isles and was founded in 1683, 60 years before the British Museum.

The Bodleian Library—Contains 1 of the 2 largest collections of C. S. Lewis' works and manuscripts, the other being the Marion E. Wade Center at Wheaton College, Chicago. The Lewis collection at the Bodleian is located in the Western Manuscripts section and contains more than 2,000 copies of his letters and the originals, including his correspondence to Sister Penelope Lawson, Ruth Pitter, Inkling Nevill Coghill, and many others. The collection also contains original manuscripts by Lewis, including those of *A Grief Observed*, *Studies in Words*, *Letters to Malcolm: Chiefly on Prayer*, and others; plus partial manuscripts of *Surprised By Joy*, *That Hideous Strength*, *Mere Christianity*, and portions of the Narnian stories, including Lewis' original map of Narnia. The Lewis collection has all of the first editions of Lewis' works, both British and American, and most of the foreign translations, and also has a large selection of related manuscripts, papers, and memorabilia.

Lewis and his brother Warren did much reading, studying, and research in the Bodleian. In fact, it was here that Warren did the research for many of his volumes of French history. In a letter to his father in 1928, Jack wrote that the library would be "one of the most delightful places in the world" if only he could smoke and if there were upholstered chairs! The library room Lewis was writing about was the Duke Humfrey Room, which sits above the Divinity School of the Bodleian.

The Divinity School and Duke Humfrey Room are part of the Old Library, which contains the General Catalogue and reference section; subjects such as English, Theology, Classics, and History; and the Western Manuscripts section. The Divinity School is the oldest and most beautiful of the library buildings (renovated by Sir Christopher Wren). This reading room was specially built to house the great collection of books and manuscripts given to the University by Duke Humfrey of Gloucester, the younger brother of King George V.

To reach the Divinity School from Magdalen College, go up High Street to University St. Mary's Church (right), then turn right at the church on Catte Street, and go past the Radcliffe Camera (left) to the Old Schools Quad, which has a statue of the third Earl of Pembroke in its center. The

Divinity School has a delightful little gift shop and gives tours daily during the week.

The New Bodleian Library's main building is in downtown Oxford, on Parks Road across from the Clarendon Building, and dates from 1930. It contains the book stacks, which are kept underground, the Oriental and Maps sections, the Music section, and modern manuscripts. Other specialist libraries included in the Bodleian family are the 90,000-volume Indian Institute Library, the Law Library in the St. Cross building complex, the Rhodes House Library with its collections of American and African literature, and the Radcliffe Science Library.

The Bodleian Library is one of the oldest and most famous in the world. It takes it name from Sir Thomas Bodley, a diplomat who is buried in Merton College Chapel. Bodley actually refounded the library in 1598 because the earlier medieval library had been neglected and finally dispersed due to the political and religious upheavals in the 16th century. Bodley stocked the library with 2,000 books initially, and in 1610 drew up an agreement with the major printing company of the time that allowed the library a copy of every book printed.

Today the Bodleian is one of 6 libraries that receives a copy of every book printed in the U.K. It has more than 6,500,000 volumes, 973,000 maps, and nearly 91 miles of shelving—with 2 miles added each year. No book can be taken out of the Bodleian by anyone, no matter how exalted one's status. Prince Charles was once refused, as was Cromwell. Readers are admitted by ticket and must be members of the University or suitably sponsored to use the library, and reading and studying take place on the premises.

The Oxford Botanic Garden—Where C. S. Lewis often walked and met friends such as Tolkien (see p. 42) to talk and get away from the rigors of college life. One of the most inspiring sights in Oxford is the view he must have seen many times from the Botanic, looking back toward High Street and the great Magdalen Tower, which looms over everything and is "serene, majestic, powerful and reassuring."

This beautiful and very popular garden is the oldest botanic garden in England. It lies on the site of an old Jewish cemetery that was abandoned in 1290, and was founded as a "physic" garden in 1621. The garden boasts more than 150 different species of trees, including a yew planted in 1650; 8,000 plant varieties; a very old rock garden; several glass houses; and a bog garden.

The Magdalen Tower as seen from the Botanic Garden, Oxford

The old Physic Garden achieved eminence when Professor Charles Daubeny, a Darwinian evolutionist, was appointed caretaker in 1834. Daubeny changed the name to Botanic Garden and directed its studies toward botany and evolution, and at his own expense put up the laboratory that now sits on the north side of the garden in front and to the right of the entrance. It was here that he, T. H. Huxley, and others celebrated their intellectual victory over the "creationists" at the debate on Darwin's theories held at the University Museum in 1860.

Oxford Botanic Garden is located at the bottom of High Street, opposite Magdalen College and between the Cherwell River and Christ Church Meadow.

No. 1 Brewer Street, St. Aldate's—Birthplace of Dorothy L. Sayers (13 June 1893), a friend of C. S. Lewis and Charles Williams. The noted mystery writer, lay theologian, Dantean scholar, and playwright corresponded with both men about literary and religious matters.

When Dorothy was born, her home included her parents, her grandmother, an aunt (and her parrot), and several servants. She lived in Oxford till about age 5. She remembered being seen in her carriage by Professor Charles L. Dodgson ("Lewis Carroll"), who still lived in retirement at Christ Church. He died in 1898, about the time the Sayers family moved to Bluntisham, Cambridgeshire.

Dorothy was baptized across the street from her home at Christ Church Cathedral on 15 July, as shown by the Cathedral register. Dorothy's father, the Rev. Henry Sayers, was Headmaster of Christ Church Cathedral Choir School. No. 1 Brewer Street was (and is) the Headmaster's house, and now includes No. 2, which may have been added in 1893. The School is next door at No. 3; the oldest part was probably built in 1893 during the tenure of Rev. Sayers.

Brewer Street is a narrow alley that runs west from St. Aldate's, opposite the south tower of the façade of Christ Church College. Along the north side of Brewer is a section of the 13th-century medieval wall, which is now a part of Pembroke College. Nos. 1 and 2 stand on the south side of the street near the east end, are 2 stories high, made of yellow stone, and have mullioned windows and Georgian doorways.

Cowley Fathers Mission House, Marston Street—Where Lewis made regular confessions to one of the Cowley priests, Father Walter Adams (died in 1952), beginning in 1940. Lewis mentioned Father Adams in *Letters: C. S. Lewis-Don Giovanni Calabria* (1988), and considered him one of the holiest men he had ever met.

The Cowley Fathers, known locally as the "Cowley dads," is the name used for the Society of St. John the Evangelist, an Anglican religious community for men in the Church of England founded in 1866. The Fathers met in the mission house next to the Church of St. John the Evangelist, which now houses St. Stephen's House, an Anglican theological college in the Catholic tradition.

Marston Street is in the Oxford suburb of Cowley. It is located south of Magdalen College down Iffley Road (left), between Stockmore and St. James Streets, near the University Sports Centre.

Oxford Crematorium and Garden of Remembrance—Site of Joy Gresham Lewis' funeral service on Monday, 18 July 1960, following her death on 14 July. After Joy's cremation, Jack composed this memorial in her honor from a poem he had previously written for Charles Williams.

> *Remember Helen Joy Davidman*
> *D. July 1960*
> *Loved Wife of C. S. Lewis—*
> *Here the whole world (stars, water, air,*
> *And field, and forest, as they were*
> *Reflected in a single mind)*
> *Like cast-off clothes was left behind*
> *In ashes yet with hope that she,*
> *Re-born from holy poverty,*
> *In Lenten lands, hereafter may*
> *Resume them on her Easter Day.*

The Crematorium is located just beyond Bayswater Brook on Bayswater Road on the eastern outskirts of the city. Joy's memorial plaque is in the garden walkway to the back (right) of the chapel, on a pillar with several others.

Parson's Pleasure—The swimming area for men on the River Cherwell that Lewis enjoyed often as a student and later as a professor at Magdalen College. It is located north of the college near the University Parks, where the 2 branches of the river come together. Now a recreational area and park, Lewis mentioned Parson's Pleasure in *They Stand Together* and *All My Road Before Me*.

The Radcliffe Camera—Where Lewis often studied and read and also passed while on walks around the University center. The Camera ("chamber") is part of the Bodleian Library, and may be the most photographed building in Oxford. Originally known as the Radcliffe Library, it was built in 1737–1748. It is bounded by the School's Quadrangle, All Souls College, Brasenose College, and St. Mary's Church.

The building is not only beautiful but unusual in that it was the first circular library built in England. Its dome, once called "an Orthodox Easter egg," is the only one of its kind in Oxford, standing majestically among all the towers and spires. Now used exclusively for book storage and as a reading room, Radcliffe is not open to the public.

The Sheldonian Theatre—Where Lewis once attended a concert performed by the London Philharmonic Orchestra. There is a fine account in William Griffin's biography, *Clive Staples Lewis: A Dramatic Life* (1986), of an *Encaenia* ceremony in the Sheldonian, the day on which the university bestows degrees. The Theatre was also used for the brief "singing scene" in the movie *Shadowlands*.

This grand and strikingly beautiful theatre, built between 1664 and 1669, was the first major building designed by Sir Christopher Wren. He patterned it after the Theatre of Marcellus in Rome, which he knew only from pictures. The Sheldonian's purpose was to provide a place for University degree ceremonies, both earned and honorary, usually held in St. Mary's University Church. It was named for and financed by Gilbert Sheldon, Archbishop of Canterbury (1663) and a former chancellor of the university who, for some reason, refused to even look inside.

The interior of the Sheldonian is made entirely of wood, painted to look like marble. This was done to keep costs down, but also for good acoustics. Some notable features of the Theatre—not a theatre in the usual sense of the word, since no play has ever been performed here—are the ceiling painting, which represents an open sky, and the 70'x80' area of roof timbers made of enormous Baltic cedars that are totally unsupported from below. The roof is a major attraction for architects from all over the world.

The Sheldonian is located in downtown Oxford on Broad Street, near the Museum of the History of Science and Exeter College. It is used for a wide variety of ceremonies, concerts, lectures, meetings, and other special events, and is open at specified times for tours.

Churches

Holy Trinity Church, Headington Quarry—The home church of C. S. and Warren Lewis, about a mile from the Kilns. C. S. Lewis was a member here from 1930 till his death. He is buried with Warren in a single grave in the churchyard. Lewis' "adopted mother," Mrs. Janie Moore, is also buried here, in the same grave as Alice Hamilton Moore (no relation).

Grave of C. S. and Warren Lewis, Holy Trinity Churchyard, Headington

The idea of *The Screwtape Letters* came to Lewis during a service at Holy Trinity Church in 1940, and he preached in the church several times in succeeding years. On one of these occasions during Lent, 31 March 1946, he preached about the language of prayer as expressed in *The Book of Common Prayer*, something he was to write about later in the only book he wrote about prayer. Letter XII of *Letters to Malcolm: Chiefly on Prayer* refers to a conversation about prayer that Lewis had with the former Vicar, Canon Ronald E. Head (1919–1991). Canon Head was Vicar from 1952 till his retirement in 1990, and is buried in the churchyard, not far from the Lewis brothers.

Founded in 1848, Holy Trinity is located in a quiet, secluded area of a residential neighborhood near

Headington Quarry School. On the north (left, facing the pulpit) side toward the back of the church there is a brass pew marker commemorating where the Lewis brothers sat, and near it is the Narnian window, etched with scenes from the stories. The window was dedicated in July 1991 to the memory of 2 children who died in childhood, the son and daughter of George and Kathleen Howe.

Holy Trinity Church

Church of St. Cross, Holywell—The church where Lewis' friend Charles Williams worshiped often, and also the setting for Dorothy L. Sayers' Lord Peter Wimsey mystery *Busman's Honeymoon*. Several of Lewis' friends and influences are buried in the medieval cemetery next to the church, as well as many prominent Oxonians. Among these are Inklings Hugo Dyson and Charles Williams; Austin and Katharine Farrer; Stella Aldwinckle, who helped found the Socratic Club where Lewis debated; Kenneth Grahame, author of *The Wind and the Willows*, a favorite of Lewis'; the science fiction writer James Blish, who dedicated a book to Lewis; the playwright Kenneth Tynan, whom Lewis called his most brilliant student; and George S. Gordon, who was President of Magdalen College and one of Lewis' favorite teachers.

To locate St. Cross Church, go up High Street (right) from Magdalen College and turn right on Longwall. The church is a few blocks up on the right. This very old church dates to 1100, and most of the present structure dates from the 13th and 14th centuries.

Church of St. Margaret, Binsey—The little "sad" church Lewis mentioned in *All My Road Before Me* as a place he and friend A. C. Hamilton Jenkin (see Vanauken, p. 48, and Cornwall, p. 84) visited on 21 November 1922. Built sometime near 730, the Church is only 50' long and 20' wide. Its sponsor is Christ Church College. Although it is has no modern heating and is lit only by lamps and candles, it is still used regularly for worship.

Binsey is a little village a couple of miles northwest of the Oxford city centre. It can be reached by going west on Botley Road and then turning right (north) on Binsey Lane. The church is about 1/2 mile northwest of the village, at the end of a grove of Chestnut trees.

The University Church of St. Mary the Virgin, High Street— Where Lewis preached 2 of his most memorable sermons. He preached "Learning in War-Time" (22 October 1939) to "a great crowd," and "The Weight of Glory" (8 June 1941) to "one of the largest congregations ever assembled there in modern times." Both of these sermons were later published in *Transposition and Other Addresses* (1949, in the U.S. as *The Weight of Glory and Other Addresses*).

The Pulpit in St. Mary's University Church, Oxford, where C. S. Lewis preached "The Weight of Glory"

St. Mary's stands in the physical center of the old walled city of Oxford, and the university grew up around it. Since Anglo-Saxon times it was a parish church, but by the 13th century, it had become the seat of university government, academic debate, and the awarding of degrees. The Old Congregation House, built in the 1320s on the northeast side of the church, is probably the oldest surviving university building anywhere. Its upper room became the first university library. All university business was removed from the church by the middle of the 17th century, but St. Mary's remains the place where the University formally comes to worship. Its historical tradition is rich and intertwines with the history of Oxford itself.

It was here that John Wycliff denounced the religious abuses of his day, and where the "Oxford Martyrs" Latimer, Ridley, and Cranmer were tried for heresy in the middle 1500s. In 1833, John Keble preached a famous sermon here that launched the Oxford Movement (see Keble College, p. 22). In 1744, John Wesley preached a sermon denouncing the "laxity and sloth" of the senior members of the university. After this, he was asked never to preach at St. Mary's again. John Henry Newman was Vicar from 1828 to 1843. Other noted speakers have included William Temple, Austin Farrer, and Desmond Tutu.

St. Mary's is located up High Street (right) from Magdalen College, past All Souls College and Catte Street, in front of the Radcliffe Camera. It has a wonderful little book and gift shop on its north side, and the 300-year-old former parish hall on the south side (back) is now one of the best coffee shops in Oxford. For years St. Mary's has been the most visited church in England, attracting more than 300,000 people each year, in part due to its great beauty and history but also because it is, as one person said, "the holiest place in Oxford."

Bookshops

Lewis once said that "Oxford is a dangerous place for a book lover. Every second shop has something you want." He was right, and it is hoped that the visitor to Oxford will take in some of the marvelous shops listed below, all of which, and many not listed, carry works by and about C. S. Lewis and his friends.

Blackwell's, 48-51 Broad Street—Visited often by C. S. Lewis. Blackwell's is one of the greatest bookshops in the world. It has 5 branches, including the main store in the city centre next to the White Horse, an art and poster shop across the street (27 Broad), a children's store across the street (8 Broad), a music shop on Holywell, and a paperback shop across the street (23-25 Broad). The main store is huge and has a large selection of new Lewis titles downstairs, along with a wonderful theological/religion section. The staff is always knowledgeable, friendly, and courteous. Books also may be ordered from Blackwell's site on the Internet.

Dillons, William Baker House, Broad Street—Carries a large selection of books by and about Lewis. Dillons is an "upscale" new book house, with 5 floors (including the basement) of books and a friendly, (usually) young staff. The travel and children's sections are superb. The store is located up the street from Blackwell's in the city centre, on the corner of Broad and Cornmarket.

Oxford Antiques Center, the Jam Factory, Park End Street—Often contains a good selection of Lewis titles, some of which are hard to find. The Jam Factory is located near Waterfield's (below) and across from the Railway Station. It is one of the city's best and most visited antique shops, and contains two rooms of used books. The book stock constantly changes, and prices are always very low.

Thorntons of Oxford, 11 Broad Street—Perhaps the best place for the C. S. Lewis visitor to find books on Lewis and his friends. Thorntons is an old, established, family-run used bookshop. The manager collects books by and about Lewis and Tolkien, and has an amazing collection of Tolkieniana on the first floor; the Lewis books are upstairs. Its stock, unequaled in Oxford, includes foreign language titles, scarce out-of-print editions, and a fine selection of used and rare books. Books also can be ordered from the excellent Thornton's web page on the Internet. The shop is located across the street from Blackwell's on the way to Dillons.

Waterfield's Antiquarian Booksellers, 36 Park End Street—
The largest secondhand bookshop in Oxford, with more
than 100,000 books on 4 floors. Situated in an old Victorian house, Waterfield's brims with atmosphere, creaky
wooden floors, and good bargains. The shop has a good
general stock in all subjects and is especially strong in
English books of the 17th and 18th centuries and philosophy, literature, poetry, classics, and history of all periods,
including many hard-to-find journals. To reach Waterfield's from the city centre and Blackwell's, go from Broad
Street west to George Street, then turn left on New Road
(by the police station) to Park End Street (right). The shop
is near the Oxford Railway Station and the Jam Factory.

Cambridge

"Some things are beautiful beyond hope or belief . . ."

The City of Cambridge

Cambridge is a city of just over 100,000 people, with a history dating back nearly 2,000 years to Roman times when a small garrison stood on what is now called Castle Hill, northwest of the Magdalene Bridge crossing the River Cam. It is located 60 miles by road north from London and about 80 miles northeast from Oxford.

Cambridge is arguably one of the most attractive and accessible small cities in England. Considered more "pastoral," quieter, and more secluded than busier and more congested Oxford, Cambridge is very inviting and appealing to visitors. One thing that sets it apart is its compactness—a visitor can walk around and explore the historic city centre and see the old, beautiful colleges in a couple of days, unless, of course, one wants to explore more fully the individual colleges, the pubs and restaurants, the antique and book shops, and the other attractions. Also unique to Cambridge are "the Backs."

"The Backs" near Magdalene College, Cambridge

Eight of the central colleges—Darwin, Queen's, King's, Clare, Trinity Hall, Trinity, St. John's, and Magdalene—are positioned with their backs to the river, which runs through the city south to north. These colleges back on to the riverbank, giving rise to the name "the Backs." This 1,000-meter stretch with its grassy banks, old bridges, and beautiful flowers and gardens is perfect for walking tours and exploring the central city and its wonders.

Even before C. S. Lewis moved to Cambridge in January 1955, he had found many things about the city and the university he liked. After going to the university, he found its colleges charming and "intriguing," and on the whole, the town was quieter and more relaxed than Oxford. When he moved to Cambridge to teach, he discovered that the atmosphere was less formal and more hospitable than Oxford. Many visitors to Cambridge have said and written the same thing. This is not to disparage Oxford, because it, too, is a wonderful, exciting, and in many ways unique city. But Cambridge is *different*, and it is hoped that the "C. S. Lewis visitor" to Cambridge, whether first-time or veteran, will note the differences and then celebrate both places.

Cambridge University

Cambridge is a "collegiate" university like Oxford in the sense that most of its 15,000-plus students and academicians must belong to an individual college before they can become members of the University. Like Oxford, at Cambridge there is no single "campus," but rather a collection of small colleges that make up the University. All students are junior members of 1 of the 31 colleges and private halls —6 colleges are for graduates; 3 are for women only.

Much of the charm of Cambridge comes from the beauty of the many ancient buildings and the intimate character of the college courts, quadrangles, and gardens. The most picturesque colleges are the oldest, found along the river and the city centre. They are within a short walk of each other, mostly along the Backs. The colleges can be divided into 3 groups: ancient, younger, and modern. In addition, the University boasts 6 foundations whose members comprise a mixture of graduates and undergraduates. Following are the groups of colleges and their individual founding dates, and a list of the foundations.

Ancient
Peterhouse (1284)
Pembroke (1347)
Corpus Christi (1352)
St. Catharine's (1473)
Queen's (1446)
King's (1446)
Clare (1326)
Trinity Hall (1350)
Gonville and Caius (pronounced "Keys," 1348)
Trinity (Cambridge's largest, 1547)
St. John's (1511)
Magdalene (Lewis' college, 1428)
Jesus (1496)

Sidney Sussex (1596)
Christ's (1439)
Emmanuel (1584)

Younger
Downing (1800)
Girton (1869)
Newnham (1875)
Selwyn (1882)
Homerton (1894)

Modern
New Hall (1954)
Fitzwilliam (1966)
Churchill (1960)
Robinson (1981)

Foundations
Hughes Hall
Darwin College
St. Edmund's College
Wolfson College
Clare Hall
Lucy Cavendish College

Magdalene College

Magdalene (pronounced "Maudlin") College is one of the smallest in the University, and is the only ancient college that stands across the River Cam. Magdalene was founded by Benedictine monks and was once known as Buckingham College because of the gifts it received in the late 15th century from the Duke of Buckingham, who built the chapel that dates from the 1480s, and the Hall, where Lewis once lectured on Samuel Pepys.

Magdalene is perhaps best known today for the Pepys Library, which stands in the second court. The famed diarist Samuel Pepys was a Magdalene man, and left his 3,000-volume library (intact) and his own bookcases to the college on his death in 1703. Other famous names from Magdalene include Henry Dunster, first president of Harvard; Charles Kingsley, author of *The Water Babies*, a famous children's story that Lewis enjoyed; George L.

Mallory, a mountaineer; P. M. S. Blackett, a Nobel Prize winning physicist; and actor Michael Redgrave. Authors Rudyard Kipling, Thomas Hardy, and T. S. Eliot were honorary fellows of Magdalene.

In the early 1950s, Lewis, due in part to increasing age, voluminous correspondence, and opposition to some of his curriculum reforms, was beginning to grow tired of teaching at Oxford. When a special chair of Medieval and Renaissance Literature was created at Cambridge, some of Lewis' friends there, who knew of his dissatisfaction with Oxford, suggested him for the position. A person very instrumental in this decision was Lewis' longtime friend J. R. R. Tolkien, who was on the Cambridge board of electors. Lewis moved to Cambridge and Magdalene in early January 1955, although it was agreed that he could maintain his permanent residence in Oxford and commute weekly to Cambridge during term.

At Magdalene College Lewis was a university lecturer and did not have to meet students for tutorials as he did at Oxford. Two books that came out of his lectures here were *Studies in Words* (1960) and *Spenser's Images of Life* (1967). Two lectures he gave to the Cambridge Zoological Laboratory in 1956 laid the groundwork for his famous work on medieval history, *The Discarded Image* (1964), and the Cambridge University Press published *An Experiment in Criticism* (1961). He spent his time researching and writing lectures, writing letters and books, attending literary society functions and meetings, and walking along the Backs and around other scenic places in the city. As one friend put it, Lewis "tracked down most of the foot paths in and around Cambridge."

Magdalene's entrance lies tight against the east side of Magdalene Street across the Magdalene Bridge, slightly left of the city centre. Through the gate lies the First Court. Lewis' plain, paneled rooms (not open to the public) were here in the "North Range" of the Court (facing left) on the second floor of staircase 3. Magdalene's First Court has been called the best example in Cambridge of the original medieval setting of domestic life in a college.

The small, beautiful Magdalene Chapel was built in 1480, and is on the first floor of the First Court, to the right of Lewis' rooms. It was the center of Lewis' life at

Magdalene, and he prayed there almost daily at weekday morning matins at 8 o'clock, and would often walk and pray in the Fellows' Garden behind the Pepys Library before matins.

The Fellows' Garden, Magdalene College, Cambridge

In was in Magdalene Chapel, at Evensong on 29 January 1956, that Lewis preached his last sermon, "A Slip of the Tongue." He had been invited to preach by the college chaplain. The little chapel was filled to capacity, with people sitting in the aisles. "A Slip of the Tongue" was a short and intimate sermon, and at its core was really about discipleship. It dealt with Lewis' own, almost constant battle to separate the spiritual from the worldly in his life, and not to let temporal desires interfere with and weaken his spiritual life with God. In the sermon Lewis told his audience not to "dabble" with God, but rather to "take a leap of faith" and be committed Christians. "A Slip of the Tongue" was later published in *Screwtape Proposes a Toast and Other Pieces* (1965) and *The Weight of Glory and Other Addresses* (revised and expanded edition, 1980).

Chapels and Churches

Great St. Mary's, the University Church—A church where Lewis worshiped and visited several times during his tenure at Cambridge. It is located on King's Parade in the city centre, across the street from King's College Chapel.

Built in 1478, today it is used for University ceremonies and the weekly Sunday evening University sermons during term.

King's College Chapel—One of the most famous and beautiful medieval buildings in the world. Founded by King Henry VI in 1440, its superb architectural craftsmanship is considered unequaled. The poet Wordsworth called King's "an immense and glorious work of fine intelligence." The historian Rudolf Ackermann (*A History of the University of Cambridge*) noted that it "cannot be paralleled by any edifice in the world." When Lewis first visited Cambridge as a young man, he was overwhelmed by his first sight of King's. He said it was "beautiful beyond hope or belief."

King's College is located in the center of the city, on King's Parade Street. It is flanked by Queen's College (left) and Clare College (right) as you face (from the street) the Wilkins Screen and Gatehouse. By the Gatehouse there is a domed Victorian postbox, a much-loved feature.

To reach the Chapel, go through the Gatehouse entrance into the Great Court, in the center of which is a statue of Henry VI. To the center left of the Great Court lies the Tudor Hall. Straight ahead at the back of the Court is the James Gibbs Fellows Building. To the right (north) is the Chapel, which the visitor cannot possibly miss.

The Round Church (Holy Sepulchre Church)—A church where Lewis reportedly worshiped during the late 1950s. Built in 1130, it is one of only 4 round churches still in use in England today. Its Norman shape dates back to the time of the first Christians, who built circular structures around sepulchres or tombs as a symbolic way of showing their loyalty to Christ. Located on Round Church Street across from St. John's College, the Round Church is one of the most visited attractions in central Cambridge.

People

G. E. (Elizabeth) M. Anscombe—A Roman Catholic Christian whom Lewis debated at the Socratic Club in Oxford on 2 February 1948. Miss Anscombe submitted a paper to the Club that refuted a philosophical argument Lewis made in his book *Miracles* (1947). Her paper was published in the *Socratic Digest* along with Lewis' reply. Lewis later reevaluated his position and rewrote chapter 3 of *Miracles*, the only book he ever revised.

Miss Anscombe was a student of the famous philosopher Ludwig Wittgenstein in the early 1940s and attended Newnham College as a research student. She was later professor of Philosophy at Cambridge and published a number of philosophical works. Newnham College is located across the river, past Queen's Road, just off Sidgwick Avenue, in the extreme southwest section of the city centre.

Richard Ladborough—Perhaps Lewis' best friend at Cambridge. Ladborough wrote what might be the best overall summary of Lewis' life at Cambridge, an essay titled "In Cambridge." This essay was first published in July 1975 in *CSL: The Journal of the New York C. S. Lewis Society*, and later reprinted in *C. S. Lewis at the Breakfast Table and Other Reminiscences* (ed. James T. Como, 1979). Ladborough was University Lecturer in French as well as Dean and Librarian of the Pepys Library at Magdalene.

Colleges and Other Places of Interest

Girton College—Lewis' friend Kathleen Raine (born 1908) was a research fellow in the 1950s at Girton, located on the left outskirts of the city (west) on Huntingdon Road. She was an acclaimed poet and wrote a perceptive essay about Lewis in one of the first books about him, *Light on C. S. Lewis* (1965), in which she remembers their conversations about poetry and criticism. She is mentioned in the first biography about Lewis, *C. S. Lewis: A Biography* (Roger Lancelyn Green & Walter Hooper, 1974), as one of his favorite contemporary poets.

Mill Lane Lecture Hall, Mill Lane—The place where Lewis gave his famous inaugural address at Cambridge, "De Descriptione Temporum" (in a "very large tiered lecture theatre"), on Monday, 29 November 1954, his 56th birthday. Lewis was introduced by the distinguished historian G. M. Trevelyan, who mentioned to the large crowd present that Lewis' election to the University chair was the only one in his long experience in which the electing committee had voted unanimously.

"De Descriptione Temporum" was first published by the Cambridge University Press as a pamphlet (1955) and later in *They Asked for a Paper* (1962) and *Selected Literary Essays* (1969). The last part of the address was included in the film *Mere C. S. Lewis* (Episcopal Radio-TV Foundation, Atlanta GA). Both the film and an audiotape of the entire address are in print and can be ordered from the ERTVF.

To reach Mill Lane, head south from the King's College down King's Parade, which becomes Trumpington (pass St. Botolph's Church on the left). The Lane is to the right and southwest of Trumpington. The lecture hall is next door to "Old Orleons," formerly a furniture depository for a Cambridge department store called "Eaden Lily," and now is, according to a resident of Cambridge, an "American-style eating place that specializes in Southern food and provides some entertainment."

Milton Road—Residence of the H. C. Chang family whom Lewis visited in the 1950s. Chang was lecturer in Chinese at the University, and he and Lewis had written when Chang held a teaching position in Singapore. Milton Road was within walking distance of his college, just off Chesterton Road to the north of Magdalene.

Narnian lamppost, Grantchester—Thought to be Lewis' inspiration for the Narnian lamppost in *The Lion, the Witch, and the Wardrobe*, according to Dr. M. A. Manzalaoui, a retired college English professor who was Lewis' student at Oxford immediately after World War II. Manzalaoui wrote an essay on Narnia that includes a theory explaining that it came from his seeing a real lamppost that still exists near Cambridge, in a clearing in a field in Newnham, between the river and the pathway to Grantchester. (For the complete essay, see the excellent *Journey into Narnia* by Kathryn Lindskoog [Hope Publishing, 1998]).

Grantchester is a pretty little village 2 miles south of Cambridge. It is famous for being the home of the poet Rupert Brooke. The houses where he lived from 1910 to 1912, the Orchard and the Old Vicarage, remain. In Victorian days nighttime skating was a favorite pastime, and the lamppost was placed in the field to illuminate the "skating rink." Manzalaoui asserts that this lamppost was once known to many academicians, and that Lewis probably knew about it. He loved to walk around the many picturesque footpaths and woods of Cambridge, and also liked to ice skate on the pond in his woods behind his home, the Kilns (see p. 34) in Oxford. Many scholars believe that these woods were Lewis' inspiration for the Narnian woods, and Manzalaoui believes that the "lonely lamppost in a clearing in Narnia was inspired by the lonely lamppost in a clearing near Cambridge."

To reach the lamppost from the Cambridge city centre, travel south on Queen's Road (behind the Backs), turn right on the Fen Causeway, and then right (south) on Trumpington Road. Follow the road past Long Road until it becomes High Street. Look for a sign pointing right (west) to Byron's Pool. Follow the path toward the Pool. Look for a field surrounded by trees that appears to be a clearing in the woods.

St. John's Street—Where Barbara Reynolds, a fellow academician, lived in the 1950s when she was University lecturer in Italian Literature. On one occasion Lewis met her 6-year-old daughter, who had recently enjoyed hearing a reading of *The Lion, the Witch, and the Wardrobe* but was concerned about Edmund's safety and was a little frightened. When Mrs. Reynolds introduced Lewis to her daughter, the little girl said, "Well, he looks as though he'd make it come all right." In 1955, Lewis returned again to Mrs. Reynolds' flat on St. Johns, this time to take part in a discussion group. St. John's Street runs in front of Trinity College (see below) from Trinity Street.

Trinity College—The place where Lewis gave the Clark Lectures (1944), which were the basis for his monumental *English Literature in the Sixteenth Century Excluding Drama* (1954), later titled *Poetry and Prose in the Sixteenth Century*. In February 1961, at the request of Mrs. Barbara Reynolds, the noted Dantean scholar and later biographer of Dorothy L. Sayers, Lewis lectured to the Cambridge Dante Society in the Guest Room at Trinity.

Trinity is Cambridge's largest college, located in the city centre on Trinity Lane down and to the right of King's College. Its intellectual tradition and architectural splendor make it one of the most visited colleges in the University. Its Great Court, with more than 2 acres of lawns and paths, is the largest college court in either Oxford or Cambridge. The Court was the original scene of the traditional "Great Court Run," a race around the court while the clock strikes 12, featured in the film *Chariots of Fire* (although the film was made at Eton College).

University Library—The location of the tower (156' tall) described in Lewis' *The Dark Tower and Other Stories* (1977). *The Dark Tower* is set in Cambridge, and is supposedly an unfinished addition to Lewis' famed space novels *Out of the Silent Planet, Perelandra*, and *That Hideous Strength*. There has been much scholarly debate in Lewis circles about whether or not he wrote this story. Many competent scholars now admit that if Lewis was indeed the author of *The Dark Tower*, it was his worst effort. There seems to be good evidence that Lewis was not the author, although opinion is still out on who the real author was and why the book was written.

The library is located west of the Backs, between Robinson College on Grange Road and Queen's Road. It is almost directly opposite Trinity Hall, Clare, and King's colleges.

Westcott House—An Anglican training college where Lewis had a memorable discussion (1959) with some ministers and theologians about the New Testament and the miraculous. Lewis was perturbed that a book of sermons by the well-known Anglican theologian Alex Vidler contained an essay that essentially called Jesus' miracle at the wedding of Cana a "parable." Always the evangelist, Lewis thought that if the Church of England abandoned belief in the miraculous—a position the "worldwide church" had held for 2,000 years—this would cause the theologically uneducated to abandon the faith.

Westcott is located in the city centre on Jesus Lane opposite Jesus College and next to All Saints Church, one of the most significant Gothic Revival buildings in England.

Pubs and Restaurants

The Blue Boar Inn—A favorite of Lewis where he often stayed and housed guests. This inn stands at the site of the old Blue Boar Hotel. A very popular restaurant today (open for lunch only), it is located at 17 Trinity Street, almost directly across from Trinity College.

The Pickerell Inn—Lewis' favorite pub in Cambridge. Built in the 16th century, the Pickerell sits directly across the street from the entrance to Magdalene College.

Bookshops

Heffers on Trinity Street—Carries many new Lewis books, and its children's store always stocks a selection of the Narnian books. One of the official University booksellers.

Dillons on Sydney Street—Second only to Heffers, boasts an impressive stock of books by and about Lewis.

The Haunted Bookshop—Has perhaps the city's best selection of used Lewis books and books by George MacDonald, J. R. R. Tolkien, and others. The owners, Sarah Key and Phil Salin, are extremely knowledgeable about Lewis, and are always willing to help. It is located in St. Edward's Passage, directly across from the entrance to King's College.

G. David—Near the Haunted Bookshop.

Deighton Bell—Located on Trinity Street.

Green Street Bookshop—Located on Green Street in the city centre.

Galloway and Porter—Located on Green Street in the city centre.

The Bookshop on Magdalene Street—Has one of the city's best selections of used religious works, including Lewis'. Across from Magdalene College next to the Pickerell Inn.

England

"I suppose I reached as much happiness as is ever to be found on this earth."

Walking Tours

C. S. Lewis always loved to walk, and he spent many happy hours on solitary walks and "tramping together" with his brother Warren and other friends in the glorious English, Welsh, and Irish countrysides. From the 1920s until 1939, he and some friends would put on old clothes and pack sandwiches and smokes in their rucksacks and venture off, often walking up to 50 miles a week and staying overnight in old-fashioned pubs and inns. Lewis' diary *All My Road Before Me* contains many details of his walks. In *The Four Loves* ("Friendship"), he called these times with friends "the golden sessions" and one of the most wonderful gifts of life.

In a letter to Arthur Greeves, Lewis told about a special 50-mile walking tour he took in April 1930, with friends Owen Barfield, A. C. Harwood, and Walter Field. The walk started in Dunster, Somerset, and then turned west to Luccombe, south to Dunkery Beacon Hill, north through Stoke Pero and Wilmersham Farm, west to Lynmouth, and then south to Challacombe in Exmoor, southwest England.

Most of the tour was through what is now Exmoor National Park, known for its beautiful and often uninhabited landscapes, bare hills of heather and grass, picturesque villages and hamlets with beautiful old churches, and abundance of deer and other wild animals. Dunster (population 800) is a particularly attractive village, dominated by its partly medieval castle, which dates back to Norman times. Dunkery Beacon has always been a good base for walks, and upon reaching the top of the hill, Lewis wrote that "we could find nothing higher." The tiny hamlet of Stoke Pero was noted for its "little grey church without a tower that holds only about 20 people." The Exmoor farms were "some of the loveliest habitations you can imagine."

After walking down the Lynn Valley and through the Valley of Rocks, which Lewis did not enjoy because of the absence of water, the tour made its way through the scenic and wild inland moors (open and uncultivated land, often covered with heather) to Challacombe. Upon reaching the tiny village (not listed in many current guides), Lewis wrote, "We had done over 20 miles and felt immortal." A more complete survey of this tour, complete with wonderful pictures of the countryside, is found in *C. S. Lewis: Images of His World*.

In his diary *Brothers and Friends*, Warren Lewis chronicled and described several of the 8 annual walking tours he and Jack took. They are as follows.

1-4 January 1931, "54 miles across the Wye Valley"—Warren wrote that this walking tour, his first, was "so full and pleasant," he did not have time to record it in his journal. He and Jack visited the gorgeous Gloucester Cathedral (pronounced "Gloster") on the way south to Chepstow, then continued on over the Wye River to Monmouth, Ross, and Hereford, passing Tintern (see p. 90) and visiting St. Briavels Castle on the way (inhabited by the aunt of a student of Lewis'). Monmouth (population 7,500), located on the Welsh side of the English border, is noted for its beautiful and unique 13th-century stone-gated bridge.

3-6 January 1933, "continuing their ascent of the Wye Valley"—Warren did not mention the details of this tour in *Brothers and Friends*, nor did Jack in his published letters to Arthur Greeves and other collections of letters.

1-6 January 1934, "continuing along the Wye Valley into Wales"—Warren described this tour in great length in *Brothers and Friends*. On it he and Jack were accompanied by Mrs. Janie Moore and her daughter Maureen. The tour began in Hereford on the Wye River, then went west to Builth, then across the river north to the little village of Newbridge-on-Wye, where Jack had visited the previous year. From the group headed north to the village of Rhayader, where Warren commented "it was not an easy town to get out of," then still north to the hamlet of Pant-y-Dwr (now on road B4518). On the fourth day of the tour the group traveled in mostly open country, again crossing the river west to Ponterwyd. The next day the tour (by bus in a driving rainstorm) went further west to Aberystwyth, Dyfed, on the west central coast of Wales. Aberystwyth (population 9,000) is now a popular seaside resort and the home of the University of Wales. When the group visited the University, Jack asked directions to the library, located in the northeast section of the city. Here they found a copy of a book by Owen Barfield and one of Jack's papers.

3-5 January 1935, "in the Chiltern Hills"—The Chilterns are located between Oxford and London, and stretch from Reading, Berkshire, about 40 miles northeast across southern Buckinghamshire. They have long been a favorite of walkers. Their most attractive area lies due south of High Wycombe, about 25 miles south of Oxford. Neither Warren nor Jack gave details of this tour in their writings, although in *Brothers and Friends* Warren mentioned a previous 2-week holiday to the Chilterns in 1933. They stayed at Flint Hall, a farmhouse in Hambledon.

13-16 January 1936, "Derbyshire"—This area is about 100 miles north of Oxford in the Peak district, near Nottingham. It is a wonderful region to visit—full of national parks, pretty villages, and historic sites. One can easily understand why the Lewis brothers chose this area; it has some of the wildest and most beautiful scenery in England. In *Brothers and Friends*, Warren recorded a visit to the village of Taddington, southeast of Sheffield, and to the church there.

5-9 January 1937, "in Dulverton, Somerset"—The village of Dulverton (population 1,300) is located south of the moor in the Barle Valley, a few miles south of the Dunkery Beacon Hill (see p. 76) of the Exmoor region where the Lewis brothers visited in 1930.

10-14 January 1938, "in Wiltshire, 51 miles"—Although the Lewis brothers did not record the details of this tour, the area was one of their favorite places in England. It contains many sites they loved and visited often, including Stonehenge and the Salisbury Cathedral.

2-6 January 1939, "in the Welsh marshes, 42 miles; also Malvern"—The Lewis brothers loved this area and visited here often, it being near Hereford and Gloucester. Malvern, Worcestershire, consists of several small towns in the Malvern Hills, which overlook the Severn Valley. Malvern was also dear to the Lewis brothers because they both attended Malvern College, Warren from 1909 to 1913, and Jack in 1912. In *Surprised By Joy*, Jack called it "Wyvern." Although Jack's time at Malvern was less enjoyable than Warren's, he came to love the beautiful college and the area around it. Again in *Surprised By Joy*, Jack described one of his teachers at Malvern, Henry Wakelyn Smith ("Smewgy"), referred to as one of his two greatest teachers, the other being Arthur T. Kirkpatrick. Jack's former student, friend, and later biographer George Sayer taught at the college from 1949 to 1974, and still lives in Malvern.

Cathedrals and Churches

Durham Cathedral and the University of Durham, Durham —Visited by the Lewis brothers in February 1944. Warren mentioned the Cathedral and city of Durham in *Brothers and Friends*. He wrote that the Cathedral was one of the most splendid Norman buildings he had ever seen, with "honey-coloured stone, twin towers at the west end, and a great central tower." The Cathedral has been called the most complete and spectacular example of Norman architecture in existence. Matthew Arnold once wrote that even Oxford had no view to compare with it.

The foundations of the Cathedral were laid in 1093. The church was completed in 1133, and 4 major additions, the Galilee Chapel, the Chapel of Nine Altars, the western towers, and the central tower, were added between 1170 and 1490.

Jack gave the Riddell Memorial Lectures for the University, actually delivered at Newcastle-Upon-Tyne, on 3 successive nights in February 1943. These were later published as *The Abolition of Man: Reflections on Education with Special Reference to the Teaching of English in the Upper Forms of Schools*. This small book is regarded as one of Lewis' most important. In it he discussed objective (moral) values and the Natural Law, which he called the "Tao."

The city of Durham (population 83,000) is located 260 miles north of London and about 75 miles from Leeds.

Lincoln Cathedral, Lincoln, Lincolnshire—Thought by Lewis to be the best cathedral he had ever seen. He described it in unpublished letters to Arthur Greeves in 1934. The original city of Lincoln was once called Lindum Colonia. Built in 47 A.D., it was one of the 4 regional capitals of Roman Britain. The city's Norman cathedral was built in 1092, and is now the third largest church in England. The city is located in central England, about 145 miles north of London.

Salisbury Cathedral, Salisbury, Wiltshire—Visited by Warren Lewis in May 1931, and by he and Jack in August of that year. Jack's friend, the famed mystery writer and lay theologian Dorothy L. Sayers, attended the Godolphin School in Salisbury (1909), and was confirmed in Salisbury Cathedral the next year.

The Lewis brothers were impressed with the "symmetry," grandeur, and grace of the much celebrated cathedral. Established in 1220, its spire—404 feet—is the tallest in England. On the north aisle there is a fascinating clock dating back to 1386, possibly the oldest in Europe. The library contains a rare original copy of the Magna Carta. The Cathedral grounds are enhanced by The Close (the largest in England), a beautiful and peaceful area of grounds, gardens, and old, impressive Georgian buildings.

Salisbury is the only city in Wiltshire. Located in extreme south-central England, it is about 130 miles west of London. The Cathedral dominates the city, sitting in its south-center, near the river Avon. The Lewis brothers often visited the Red Lion pub on their trips to Salisbury. A medieval pub that was once a coaching inn, the Red Lion may have housed the draughtsmen who worked on the cathedral. The Red Lion can be found on Milford Street in the center of the city.

York Cathedral (York Minster), York, North Yorkshire—Visited by Warren Lewis on 23 February 1943. For more than 1,300 years, worship has been taken in York Minster. It is Europe's largest medieval cathedral and one of the world's great and most inspiring buildings. The Minster is the seat of the Archbishop of York, the person second in ecclesiastical status only to the Archbishop of Canterbury. The Minster is in the north center of the city, which is about 195 miles north of London.

Schools and Colleges

Cherbourg School, Malvern, Worcestershire—A preparatory school Jack Lewis attended from January 1911 till 1913 after leaving Campbell College, Belfast. Lewis called the school "Chartres" in *Surprised By Joy*. Its enrollment at the time he attended was about 20 boys from ages 8 to 12. Cherbourg's Headmaster was Arthur C. Allen, who moved the school to Wood Norton, Evesham, in 1925. The original building, now called "Ellerslie," still stands on Abbey Road in Malvern.

University of Manchester, Manchester, Greater Manchester
—Where Lewis received the Degree of Doctor of Letters on 13 May 1959. The Presenter of the Degree, Professor R. A. C. Oliver, said of Lewis: "As a scholar he is distinguished beyond all others in his field by the extraordinary range of his knowledge . . . and the penetrating brilliance of his insight. . . . The good rather than the fashionable has been his standard."

Manchester is about 200 miles north of London, and the University lies to the south of the city centre on Oxford Street/Road.

University of St. Andrew's, St. Andrews, Fife, Scotland—
Where Lewis received an honorary Doctor of Divinity degree. The degree ceremonies were held at St. Mary's College on 8 April 1946. The famous theologian D. M. Baillie gave the laureation address for Lewis. In it he mentioned that "it is not very frequently that the University confers its Doctorate of Divinity upon a lay theologian, but it may well be proud to give this acknowledgment to the work of Mr. C. S. Lewis."

It was also at St. Andrew's that J. R. R. Tolkien gave his Andrew Lang lecture titled "On Fairy Stories" on 8 March 1939. This famous talk was later published in a more complete form in *Essays Presented to Charles Williams* (1947), a work Lewis edited and promoted as the Inklings' tribute to their great friend.

The city of St. Andrews (population 10,600) lies on the North Sea in eastern Scotland near Dundee, about 65 miles north of Edinburg. St. Mary's is in its eastern center.

Wynyard School, Watford, Hertfordshire—The first English
school the Lewis brothers attended. Warren was at Wynyard from 1905 to 1909, and Jack from 1909 to 1910. They both hated Wynyard. Jack called it "Belsen" (a Nazi death camp) in *Surprised By Joy*. Watford is about 30 miles northeast of London and almost due east of Oxford. It stood on the site of 99 Langley Road until 1992, when it was demolished.

Other Places of Interest

Boscombe, Wiltshire—Visited by Lewis in 1931. This town is located about 7 miles slightly northeast of the great cathedral city of Salisbury on Highway 338. In *They Stand Together*, Lewis wrote that its primitive church was the smallest one he had ever visited up till that time.

Bournemouth, Dorset—Where J. R. R. Tolkien and his wife Edith vacationed from time to time. They lodged at the Hotel Miramar, and Edith came to love this old Victorian seaside resort, especially for the friends she made here and the sea and climate.

In 1968, the Tolkiens moved to a bungalow on 19 Lakeside Road, very near the Miramar and a Catholic church where they worshiped. The Tolkiens' parish church was St. Joseph's (Parkstone Parish) on Bournemouth Road. They worshiped here occasionally, but mostly attended Sacred Heart Church in the Richmond Hill section of the city because of their friendship with Denis Tolhurst, the doctor at Sacred Heart.

At their Lakeside Road residence, for the first time the Tolkiens enjoyed central heating, separate bathrooms, and a new kitchen. The garage was converted into a study and an office, where Tolkien had the luxury of a secretary provided for him by his publisher.

After a short illness, Mrs. Tolkien died at age 82 at a nursing home in Bournemouth on 29 November 1971, the same month and day of C. S. Lewis' birth in 1898. Her husband died here less than two years later on 2 September 1973, after a visit with Dr. and Mrs. Tolhurst at their home on Talbot Avenue, Talbot Woods.

Bournemouth is a little more than 100 miles southwest of London, near Southampton. The Hotel Miramar is located on Grove Road, East Cliff, which is in the southeast section of the city between Gervis Road and East Overcliff Drive.

Boxgrove, West Sussex—The home of Rev. Peter W. Bide (born 1912), who attended lectures by Lewis while a student at Oxford (1936–1939), and later became his good friend. Rev. Bide performed the marriage ceremony of Jack and Joy Lewis at the Churchill Hospital, Oxford, on 21 March 1957. At the ceremony Rev. Bide laid hands on Joy and offered a prayer of healing. Soon after the marriage, her cancer was in remission, and she lived another 3 years. Boxgrove is 23 miles west of Brighton, near Chichester.

56 Ravenswood Road and Clifton College, Bristol, Wiltshire

—The home of C. S. Lewis' "adopted mother" Mrs. Janie King Moore (1872–1951) from 1907 to 1929. Mrs. Moore met C. S. Lewis in June 1917, when she and her daughter Maureen lived in Oxford. Mrs. Moore's son, Edward Frances Courtenay ("Paddy"), had joined the Officer's Training Corps in preparation for World War I and was sent to Keble College, Oxford, where he met Lewis and the two became friends. After Paddy was killed early in the war, Lewis became friends with the Moores. Later they became part of his "surrogate family" in Oxford.

Bristol, southwestern England's largest city (population 414,000), is due west of and about 118 miles from London. Ravenswood Road is in the Redlands section of Bristol, near the city centre. Paddy Moore was a pupil at Clifton College (32 College Street) in the northwest suburbs of the city, and his name is 1 of 600 inscribed on the Memorial Gateway of the college to honor those from Bristol who died in their country's service in World War I.

Carmarthen, Carmarthenshire, Wales

—The site of Lewis' address titled "Christian Apologetics," delivered at Easter in 1945. His address was read to an assembly of Anglican priests and youth leaders. Ironically, Carmarthen, a town in western Wales, near Swansea, is widely believed to have been the birthplace of Merlin the Magician from the Arthurian legends, a figure prominently featured in Lewis' *That Hideous Strength* (1945). "Christian Apologetics" was later published in *Christian Reflections* (1967), and is one of Lewis' most widely known and praised essays.

Cirencester, Gloucestershire

—Visited by Lewis just before his death in 1963. Here he heard a first performance of Donald Swann and David Marsh's *Perelandra*. The opera libretto was performed at a country house, and Lewis enjoyed it so much that he was moved to tears by the performance. Mr. Swann later wrote music for J. R. R. Tolkien's poems called *The Road Goes Ever On* (published 1967), based on *The Lord of the Rings* trilogy and *The Adventures of Tom Bombadil*.

Cirencester (population 13,500) is located about 15 miles west of Oxford in the Cotswolds. It is known for its Roman history, the "old world" beauty and charm of its homes and markets, and St. John's Church, one of England's largest churches.

Coln St. Aldwyn, Gloucestershire—A little village Jack and Warren visited in December 1945. It lies east of Oxford near Fairford in the Cotswolds, and was called "a dream village" by Warren in *Brothers and Friends*.

Cornwall—The birthplace and home of C. S. Lewis' University College friend A. K. Hamilton Jenkin (1900–1980). Jenkin was born in Redruth, where his family had lived since the 18th century. Lewis' diary *All My Road Before Me* gives many details of their friendship. He mentioned in *Surprised By Joy* that Jenkin was his first lifelong friend. In Cornwall, Jenkin lived at St. Ives, where he was a journalist, broadcaster, and historian. He wrote several books about his beloved Cornwall, including *The Story of Cornwall* and *Cornwall and Its People*.

Fairford, Gloucestershire—Where the Lewis brothers visited in September 1945. Warren Lewis recorded in *Brothers and Friends* that it was "one of the loveliest villages" he had ever seen. They especially admired the old stone houses ("every house is a gem"). Later in the year Warren visited Fairford again, this time with his friend J. R. R. Tolkien.

Fairford is in the beautiful Cotswolds area of southeast England, near the much visited towns of Bibury and Cirencster. It is about 13 miles west of Oxford, and a few miles west of Kelmscott, the home of Victorian poet, novelist, and designer William Morris, whose *The Well at the World's End* (1896) was a particular favorite of Lewis'.

Farnham, Surrey—The home of Pauline Diana Baynes (born 1922), the illustrator for *The Chronicles of Narnia*. An internationally known artist, she also illustrated J. R. R.

Tolkien's *The Adventures of Tom Bombadil* and *Smith of Wootton Major* and more than 100 other children's books. In 1967, Miss Baynes won the prestigious Kate Greenaway Medal for her illustrations in Grant Uden's *Dictionary of Chivalry*. Her most recent work includes illustrations for Brian Sibley's *Land of Narnia* (1990) and *A Book of Narnians* (1994, with text by James Riordan). A widow, Miss Baynes lives at Rock Barn Cottage, Dockenfields, Farnham, in the North Downs area of Surrey.

Great Bookham, Surrey—Where C. S. Lewis' tutor Arthur T. Kirkpatrick (1848–1921) lived from 1900 until the time of his death. Lewis was sent to Great Bookham in 1914 to be prepped for Oxford. In *Surprised By Joy*, he described Kirkpatrick (known affectionately at "the Great Knock") as "a Presbyterian and was now an atheist . . . a 'Rationalist' of the old, high and dry 19th-century type." Lewis was taught by Kirkpatrick to think clearly and logically, and he learned to love debate and logical argument for the rest of his life.

Great Bookham is located just south of London, near Leatherhead. The Kirkpatrick home, "Gastons," was demolished years ago, and the remnants of an old barn are all that exist today.

"The Farm," Huntly, Aberdeenshire, Scotland—The birthplace of George MacDonald (1824–1905), whose work *Phantastes* triggered C. S. Lewis' spiritual awakening ("baptized my imagination"), which led years later to conversion. Lewis once wrote that, other than the Bible, MacDonald's *Lilith* moved him spiritually more than any other book, that MacDonald was "his master," and that he knew of no other writer who was closer to the spirit of Christ.

MacDonald was a man of multifaceted depth—a sometimes controversial theologian, spiritual mystic, poet, novelist, preacher, essayist, highly acclaimed lecturer (he once toured and lectured in the U.S. to enthusiastic crowds), actor, scientist, editor, and fantasy writer. He wrote more than 50 books, 30 of them novels that sold millions of copies, most after his death. Many of his books are still in print. His tales such as *The Princess and Curdie*, *At the Back of the North Wind*, and *Sir Gibbie* continue to delight children of all ages, including adults.

MacDonald's gift for writing timeless fantasy with explicit Christian ideas influenced and deeply affected many in his time and continues to do so today. He was held in high esteem by his own contemporaries such as Tennyson, Ruskin, Thackery, and Trollope, and was good friends with Charles Dickens and Lewis Carroll. His writings about imagination impressed Tolkien, the poet W. H. Auden described him as "one of the most remarkable writers in the 19th century," and G. K. Chesterton claimed that MacDonald's *The Princess and the Goblin* "changed his whole existence."

MacDonald spent his early childhood, from 1825 to 1837, at "the Farm," a 3-story Georgian-style country house built by his father and uncle. The Johannesen family recently acquired the home, which is now open to visitors during special times of the year. With its 3 bedrooms and a private kitchen, it can accommodate guests. There is also a "growing collection" of MacDonald's works available for reading in the sitting-room library.

Huntly is about 35 miles northwest of Aberdeen, just off the main A96 road. For further information about the places of George MacDonald, many of which are in Scotland, consult these excellent biographies:

- Michael R. Phillips, *George MacDonald—Scotland's Beloved Storyteller* (Minneapolis MN: Bethany House, 1987)
- William Raeper, *George MacDonald* (Batavia IL: Lion Publishing, 1987)
- Rolland Hein, *George MacDonald: Victorian Mythmaker* (Nashville TN: Star Song Publishing, 1993)

For more information and booking, contact:

Debbie Jo Johannesen
P.O. Box 24
Whitehorn CA 95589
707-986-7465
(fax) 707-986-1656
(e-mail) johannesen@humboldt.net

Seth Johannsen
The Farm
Huntly, Scotland AB54 4QY
011-44-1466-792816

Lane End, Buckinghamshire—Where Jack first conceived of his classic *The Great Divorce* (1945), according to George Sayer's *Jack: C. S. Lewis and His Times*. On Thursday, 13 April 1933, while on holiday at a farmhouse in the Chilterns (see p. 77), Warren and Jack went out to explore the area around the villages of Skermilt and Frieth. While passing through Frieth, they saw a notice of a Passion Play to be performed the next day (Good Friday) in the church at the village of Lane End, just up the road north from Frieth, near High Wycombe. The brothers, along with Mrs. Moore and Maureen, attended the play. On Sunday they attended the Easter communion service at the little church. It was at this church where Jack's idea for his book came about.

Long Crendon, Buckinghamshire—A pretty little village about 10 miles northeast of Oxford where Lewis' great friends Owen Barfield and Ruth Pitter lived. Barfield (1898–1998) met Lewis in 1919 while a student at Wadham College, Oxford. After his marriage in 1923, Barfield moved to Long Crendon where he lived for several years. A member of the Inklings, Barfield taught Lewis much about religion and philosophy. Lewis called him "the wisest and best of my unofficial teachers." Barfield's most famous book was *Poetic Diction* (1928 and still in print), which had a profound effect on Lewis and J. R. R. Tolkien.

Ruth Pitter (1898–1992) was converted in World War II while listening to Lewis' radio broadcasts that later became *Mere Christianity*. They met after she wrote and thanked him for his talks and books, and they became close friends thereafter. Lewis once told a friend that if he were a marrying man, Ruth would have been the person he would have chosen to marry. Many people believe that Lewis would have married Ruth even after his wife Joy's death, except for his own poor health. A very accomplished poet, Miss Pitter was a published poet at age 13, and was the first British woman to win the Queen's Medal for poetry. Among her many works are *Urania*, *A Mad Lady's Garland*, and *A Trophy of Arms*—for which she won the Hawthendorn Prize (1936).

Minster Lovell, Oxfordshire—Visited by Lewis and some friends on 20 June 1963, not long before his death. They dined at the Old Swan Hotel. This exceptionally pretty little village sits on the banks of the River Windrush in the Cotswolds and is about 9 miles west of Oxford. It is noted for its fine old bridge and its homes with an even mixture of Cotswold stone and thatch. Minster Lovell's church was built in 1431 on the foundations of an earlier 12th-century church. Behind it stands the often-visited ruin of Minster Lovell Hall, originally a fortified manor house.

Old Cleve, Somerset—Where Lewis spent "the happiest 4 weeks" of his life. In *They Stand Together* (letter 103) and *All My Road Before Me*, Lewis mentioned staying for a month in this cottage "smothered in flowers." He wrote that this little village was not far "from the end of the world." From his cottage he could see "black mountains" (probably the Brendon Hills to the south) and across the water (Bridgewater Bay) "the hazy outline of Wales."

Old Cleve is a tiny hamlet near the village of Washford, east of Dunster (see p. 76). It is shown on a map accompanying the details of this tour in *C. S. Lewis: Images of His World.*

Rycote Chapel, Thame, Oxfordshire—Where the Lewis brothers often visited and took friends. Lewis' good friend and taxi driver Clifford Morris worked here in his later years, giving tours and providing information to visitors. Queen Elizabeth also worshiped here some as a child. Built in 1449, the Chapel is located a few miles east of Oxford on the A329 Road, near Long Crendon.

St. Albans, Hertfordshire—Where C. S. Lewis' great friend and Inkling Charles Williams lived for several years of his childhood and early teens before moving to London to work for Oxford University Press. At age 5, Williams was confirmed at St. Albans Abbey, and on 12 April 1917, was married to Florence Conway at the Abbey. Built in 1077, the Abbey was later named a cathedral.

The Williams family lived at No. 15 (now No. 36) Victoria Street in the center of the town east of the Cathedral. Charles attended the Abbey School on Spicer Street (now Abbey Mill Lane). The school (next to the Cathedral) was once the town jail, and is now housed in the Abbey Gateway and called St. Albans School. St. Albans, now affluent and with a population of 77,000, is about 25 miles northwest of London. This very old cathedral town overlooks a site once called "Verulamium" by the Romans, whose theatre and parts of the ancient wall can still be seen in the southwest parts of the city.

Convent of the Community of St. Mary the Virgin, Wantage, Oxfordshire—The home of Lewis' good friend Sister Penelope Lawson CSMV (1890–1977). She was a nun and librarian at this old Anglican convent, founded in 1848. She entered the Convent in 1912, and first wrote Lewis in 1939, expressing her appreciation for *Out of the Silent Planet*. This letter began a friendship and correspondence that lasted for many years. Both exchanged books (Penelope wrote, edited, and translated more than 25), advice, and encouragement. Lewis and Penelope met in 1942, when he was invited to lecture on theology to the nuns at the Convent. He later dedicated his second space novel, *Perelandra* (1943), "to some ladies at Wantage." When the Portuguese edition of the book was released, the dedication had been translated "to some wanton ladies." Wantage (population 9,700) is about 15 miles south of Oxford.

Stephen Langdon Inn, Shere, Surrey—An inn Lewis visited as a young man, described in a letter (4 October 1916) to his friend Arthur Greeves. The original inn dated from the time of Stephen Langdon (died 1228), Archbishop of Canterbury, for whom it was named. The rebuilt, "ravishing" inn is located on the A25 Road in an area known as Friday Street in the beautiful countryside between Guildford and the rural district of Dorking (east), a few miles south of London near Gatwick Airport. Lewis said this area had a "certain tinge of Alice and Wonderlandism about it." According to the *England Blue Guide*, Shere has been called "the prettiest village in Surrey."

Stonehenge—A famous archeological site visited by Lewis several times in his early years, including once on 8 April 1925. A picture of Lewis sitting at the ancient monument is in *Brothers and Friends*. In an unpublished letter (1915) from Lewis to Arthur Greeves in *C. S. Lewis: Images of His World*, Lewis speculated about the origins of Stonehenge. This famous ancient structure is located in the middle of the 100,000-acre Salisbury Plain, directly north of Salisbury.

Tintern Abbey, Monmouthshire, Wales—An ancient Cistercian abbey (established 1131) that Jack Lewis called one of the holiest places he had ever seen. After Jack and Warren's first walking tour, Lewis wrote to Arthur Greeves that "the sweetness and peace . . . cannot be imagined."

Now partially demolished, the Abbey still attracts a large number of visitors every year. It is located in southeast Wales, in the Wye Valley, on the right bank of the river Wye at the south end of the village of Tintern. The Abbey sits off road A466, 5 miles north of Chepstow and 11 miles south of Monmouth.

Whipsnade Wild Animal Park, Whipsnade, Bedfordshire—A site Lewis visited many times. In his day the park was known as Whipsnade Zoo. It is a branch of the London Zoo and was originally established to breed endangered species in captivity. It now houses 2,500 animals on a 600-acre site. Lewis' most famous visit here was on 28 September 1931, when, after a 50-mile ride in the sidecar of his brother Warren's motorcycle, he was finally intellectually convinced of the truth of the Gospel accounts of Jesus. When he had set out to the zoo from Oxford, he did not believe that Jesus was the son of God, but when he reached Whipsnade, he did. Lewis wrote in *Surprised by Joy* that this realization "was like when a man, after a long sleep, still lying motionless in bed, becomes aware that he is now awake." Whipsnade is about 50 miles from Oxford (east) near Dunstable.

Woburn Abbey and Park, Woburn, Bedfordshire—Woburn is not an abbbey but a grand stately home built on the site of a Cistercian abbey. It has been the seat of the dukes of

Bedford for the last 350 years. In the 18th century, the home was enlarged and remodeled into a huge country mansion. It is filled with furniture, porcelain, and paintings, and has a sculpture gallery, Chinese dairy, and china room. The mansion also houses a magnificent state chamber that served as Queen Victoria's private dressing room, and the Queen's bedroom, which has to be seen to be believed. The library (book room) boasts a rare copy of John James Audubon's *Birds of America* and many other interesting and priceless books.

Woburn Abbey stands in the middle of 3,000 acres of some of the most beautiful parkland in England—a paradise for nature lovers and a sanctuary for many varieties of animals. Lewis was a great lover of nature and delighted in his visits to Woburn, especially to this park (England's largest drive-through animal preserve) with its 7 miles of private roads, where herds of deer (11 species) often wander close to walkers and cars. He also enjoyed seeing the many acres of rhododendrons and rare trees and shrubs that decorate the park, especially in the spring and early summer. Woburn is a little more than 40 miles from Oxford and exactly 43 miles north of London.

London

Ave Maria Lane—Where Charles Williams first worked when he joined Oxford University Press in 1908 to work in the Paper, Printing, and Proofreading Department. The press was located then at Amen Corner in Ave Maria Lane, in the Ludgate Hill area, near St. Paul's Cathedral. In 1924, the Press moved to Amen House in Warwick Square, off Warwick Lane, a few hundred yards away. While in London, Williams and his wife Florence ("Michal") lived in a flat at 18 Parkhill Road, very near the place where Lewis' future wife Joy would live nearly 40 years later (see below).

14 Belsize Park, Hampstead—Where Joy Gresham lived for a while in the early 1950s before she married C. S. Lewis. Joy lived across the street from old Avoca House Hotel, which has since moved to 46 Belsize Park. She also lived for a few days in the hotel annex flats at 43 Belsize Park. A few years after the old Avoca Hotel moved to another part of the city, this site housed an English language school for foreign students called the Cambridge Lodge. Next, the site was a refugee hostel called the Gold Bull Hotel before recently becoming Belsize Park Hotel.

While living in London, Joy frequently worshiped at St. Peter's Anglican church near the original hotel. She socialized often with the famed science fiction writer Arthur C. Clarke and his wife at the White Horse pub (90 Fetter Lane, just off Fleet Street) in Hampstead. Earlier in the U.S., Joy and her former husband William Lindsay Gresham had met and become friends with the Clarkes. Clarke's fanciful collection of stories called *Tales from the "White Hart"* (1957) were set in a fictitious London pub that was closely based on the White Horse, where Clarke and his friends met to discuss science fiction and space travel.

The present mock Victorian White Horse is a remarkable 3-story building with an attic, over an arcaded ground floor. It is festooned with banded brickwork and stone dressings, and there is a tall, Dutch gable to Fetter Lane and an enriched ornamental moulding over the first floor windows. Belsize Park is now a fashionable urban area in north-central London that sits above Regent's Park.

Covent Garden, St. Martin's Theatre—According to *They Stand Together*, where C. S. Lewis attended a performance of the opera *Das Rheingold* on 2 May 1933. This theatre is in the Docklands area of Covent Garden (across the river next to Soho), and is located on West Street between Litchfield Street and Cambridge Circus. It is best known today for its continual performances of Agatha Christie's *The Mousetrap*, the world's longest running play, which premiered in 1952. The play transferred from the nearby Ambassador Playhouse in 1974.

Covent Garden, Theatre Royal Drury Lane—Site of the first opera C. S Lewis attended. On 14 June 1918, at the age of 20, he attended a performance here of Richard Wagner's *The Valkyrie*. Lewis discovered the haunting and beautiful operas of Wagner early in his teens, and they were his favorite music for much of his life. *The Valkyrie* is one of the 4 dramas that compose Wagner's *Ring of the Nibelung* series. Established in 1663, the Drury Lane is one of

London's most famous and enduring theatres. The current building on Catherine Street, parallel to Drury Lane, is the fourth on this site.

St. James, Haymarket Theatre—Where Lewis attended a performance in August 1922, of *The Dover Road*, by A. A. Milne, author of the Pooh stories. Lewis called it "one of the most amusing things he had ever seen," though it "collapsed" in the third act. Built in 1720, the Haymarket boasts a long history of outstanding performers and plays, starting with Henry Fielding (*Tom Jones*), whose first satire, *Tom Thumb*, ran here in 1730. The theatre is located near the National Gallery and Trafalgar Square, between Orange Street and Suffolk Place.

King's College, University of London—Where Lewis gave the annual commemoration oration *The Inner Ring* on 14 December 1944 at the King's Strand campus. It was later published in *Transposition and Other* Addresses (in the U.S. as *The Weight of Glory*, 1949), *They Asked for a Paper* (1962), *Screwtape Proposes a Toast and Other Pieces* (1965), and *The Weight of Glory and Other Addresses* (1980).

Established in 1829, King's is the constituent college of the University, which with more than 40,000 students is Britain's largest. It has a student population of more than 12,000, of which 3,000 are graduate students. The original site of King's was the Strand campus, located in central London overlooking the Thames. It is east of Covent Garden on Strand Road near the Waterloo Bridge, Aldwych, and Drury Lane.

Lambeth Palace, Westminster—Where Lewis had his first meeting with T. S. Eliot and other scholars to revise the Psalter of *The Book of Common Prayer*. The meeting was held at this London home of the Archbishop of Canterbury in January 1959. Other meetings were held in London in April (at Lambeth), July (at Selwyn College), and September (at Lambeth). The revised edition of the Psalter was published by Cambridge University Press in 1966. It was during these conferences that Lewis and Eliot became friends, after years of disagreement over literary matters.

Lambeth Palace is not usually open to visitors, but its gardens occasionally are. It is located in central London on Lambeth Palace Road, near the Imperial War Museum (east) and next to Archbishop's Park.

National Gallery, Trafalgar Square—A world-famous art gallery that Jack Lewis visited on 28 August 1922, and Warren visited in May 1931. Jack mentioned his visit here in *All My Road Before Me*. He liked the work of Botticelli, and thought the Italian Rooms were "nothing like so boring as the English." In *Brothers and Friends*, Warren mentioned "renewing his acquaintance" with the paintings of Nicholas Poussin, the French landscape artist whose work was also admired by Jack.

St. Jude on the Hill Church—Where, in April 1945, Lewis preached one of his 6 published sermons (in a worship setting), titled "The Grand Miracle." The sermon was later published in *God in the Dock* (1970). St. Jude is located in Central Square in the Golders Green area of London (Hampstead). Golders Green is also noteworthy as having been the earthly home of Sarah Smith, a memorable heavenly inhabitant in *The Great Divorce*. In the book, Lewis has his guide George MacDonald (who is also in heaven) say about Sarah: "It's someone ye'll never have heard of. Her name on earth was Sarah Smith, and she lived at Golders Green. . . . She is one of the great ones."

In Lewis' day, Golders Green was a rather poor area, but today it is a wealthy residential suburb with a strong Jewish community. Ian Nairn, in his classic guidebook to London, says that St. Jude's great visual appeal is its magnificent steeple, which "stamps the suburb from any angle and any distance."

St. Matthew's Church, St. Matthew's Parade, Ketterling Road, Northampton—Where Lewis preached the sermon "Miserable Offenders" on 7 April 1946. The sermon was later published with slight alterations as "*Miserable Offenders*": *An Interpretation of Prayer Book Language* (the Church of the Advent, Boston) and in *God in the Dock* (1970).

In 1947, during Lent, C. S. Lewis read a series of lessons and sermons at St. Matthew's and nearby All Saints church. "Miserable Offenders" was part of the series. The curate at St. Matthew's at this time was M. M. Clarke, who has fond memories of Lewis' visit and sermon. The Reverend Dr. Clarke is still at the church as Canon and remembers that when he faltered during his sermon, Lewis was kind enough to stand up and continue it for him. Lewis' sermon was delivered at Lent Evensong, the week before his former student (Sir) John Betjeman spoke in the same church.

Northampton is slightly northwest of London, just off the M1 freeway and about 40 miles northeast of Oxford. The church is situated on Ketterling Road near Cowper Street in the northeast section of the city. Founded in 680, All Saints Church is England's largest relatively intact Saxon church. It is located in Brixworth, about 8 miles north of Northhampton.

St. Paul's Cathedral, The City—A famous church the Lewis brothers visited in summer, 1934. They were impressed by its grandeur, "perfect proportions," and "vast size."

3 Spencer Road—Birthplace of Lewis' great friend Charles Williams (20 September 1886). Spencer Road is now called Caedman Road, and is located in north London, in the Holloway district, between Shelburne and Lowman Roads.

University College, Gower Street—Where Lewis' friend Charles Williams attended school in 1903 and 1904. He studied mathematics, literature, history, and languages (especially Latin and French), but unfortunately had to drop out because of his family's lack of money. One of his professors was A. E. Housman, whose classic poem *A Shropshire Lad* (1896) made a profound impression on Jack and Joy Lewis.

University was founded in 1826, and in 1900 became part of the University of London. Gower Street is west of Regent's Park in the centre of the city, and is near Bloomsbury, where members of that famous (to some, infamous) literary group lived, including Virginia Woolf, Lytton Strachey, and Clive Bell.

Annotated Bibliography

C. S. Lewis and His Friends

Arnot, Anne. *The Secret Country of C. S. Lewis*. Grand Rapids MI: Eerdmans, 1975. For young readers. Out of print.

Barratt, David. *C. S. Lewis and His World*. Grand Rapids MI: Eerdmans, 1987. Pictorial biography. Out of print.

Carpenter, Humphrey. *Tolkien*. Boston: Houghton Mifflin, 1977. Authorized biography of J. R. R. Tolkien. Written by a fine scholar who knew the family and had access to family papers. Contains a multitude of references to the important places in the life of Tolkien and Lewis. Available in paperback.

Carpenter, Humphrey. *The Inklings*. Boston: Houghton Mifflin, 1979. The only book-length treatment of Lewis and his friends. Focuses mainly on Lewis, Tolkien, and Charles Williams. Contains many references to places in the life of Lewis and the Inklings, especially those in Oxford and the walking tours. Somewhat biased toward Tolkien, but generally a fair and well-written treatment. Still out of print in the U.S., but recently reprinted in paperback (HarperCollins) in England.

Collins, David R. *J. R. R. Tolkien: Master of Fantasy*. Minneapolis MN: Lerner Publications, 1992. For young readers.

Coren, Michael. *The Man Who Created Narnia*. Grand Rapids MI: Eerdmans, 1996. Contains many pictures of Lewis' places, including several from Belfast, Oxford, and Cambridge. Limited but accurate and concise references to places. A good book for the beginning Lewis reader and traveler.

Dorsett, Lyle W. *And God Came In*. New York: Macmillan, 1983. Published in England as *Joy and C. S. Lewis* (Harper-Collins, 1994) and in the U.S. as *A Love Observed* (Shaw,

1998) with a new preface by Dorsett. The first and best treatment of Joy Davidman Gresham. One of the most well-written books in the Lewis "canon." Contains information about the places where Joy and Jack lived and visited in London and Oxford.

Gilbert, Douglas, and Clyde S. Kilby. *C. S. Lewis: Images of His World.* Grand Rapids MI: Eerdmans, 1979. The best pictorial biography ever written about Lewis. Contains many photographs and pictures of the places and people in his life. Superb introduction and running commentary (much of it in Lewis' own words). Many of the phtographs and pictures are found nowhere else, especially those of the countryside in Ireland and England where Lewis walked and spent many of his holidays. The section on Belfast contains many pictures of Lewis' home (Little Lea) and early schools; most of these are seldom seen. Out of print, but available in libraries and used bookshops.

Gormley, Beatrice. *C. S. Lewis: Christian and Storyteller.* Grand Rapids MI: Eerdmans, 1998. For young readers.

Green, Roger Lancelyn, and Walter Hooper. *C. S. Lewis: A Biography.* New York: Harcourt Brace, 1994. The first biography about Lewis. Information gained from family papers and Lewis' diaries, letters, and manuscripts. A very useful treatment of Lewis' life. Centers on Lewis' intellectual life, particularly the section on the writing of the Narnian stories. Available in paperback.

Gresham, Douglas H. *Lenten Lands.* New York: Macmillan, 1988. Memoir written by Joy Gresham Lewis' youngest son. Contains many references to the Oxford places in the life of Joy and Jack. Especially valuable for memories and anecdotes about Lewis' home, the Kilns. Available in paperback.

Griffin, William. *Clive Staples Lewis: A Dramatic Life.* San Francisco: Harper & Row, 1986. Surveys Lewis' life chronologically, beginning with 1925, when he was installed as a fellow at Magdalen College. Combines letters and quotes with commentary into a narrative format that resulted in a work containing hundreds of "scenes" from Lewis' life. Lively reading. Out of print.

Hadfield, Mary Alice. *Charles Williams—An Exploration of His Life and Work*. New York: Oxford, 1983. The authorized and only full-scale biography of Lewis' great friend and fellow Inkling Charles Williams. Contains many references to key places in Williams' life, including the Oxford University Press, where Williams was an editor.

Hooper, Walter. *Through Joy and Beyond: A Pictorial Biography of C. S. Lewis*. New York: Macmillan, 1982. A treasury of photographs and commentary on the places in the life of Lewis. Not as attractive and perceptive as Gilbert and Kilby's work, but a valuable resource for the traveler to Lewis sites in Ireland and England. Out of print.

Hooper, Walter, ed. *All My Road Before Me: The Diary of C. S. Lewis 1922-1927*. New York: Harper, 1991. Written at age 23 while an undergraduate at University College, Oxford, and an atheist. Records academic pursuits, friendships, and home life. Contains many references about visits in the countryside surrounding Oxford, and many details about his favorite places such as restaurants, pubs, and walks. A valuable resource for the Lewis traveler. Available in paperback.

Hooper, Walter. *C. S. Lewis: A Companion and Guide*. San Francisco: HarperCollins, 1996. A gold mine of information about the people and places in the life of C. S. Lewis. Includes a chronological biography; a "who's who" listing of Lewis' family, pupils, friends, spiritual mentors, and teachers; a "what's what" guide to significant places and things; a "key ideas" exploration of Lewis' thought; and overviews of Lewis' religious and literary works. Contains nothing really new, but would be a valuable addition to any Lewis traveler's library. 900-plus pages. $40.

Kilby, Clyde S., and Marjorie Mead, eds. *Brothers and Friends: The Diaries of Major Warren Hamilton Lewis*. San Francisco: Harper, 1982. Distilled from hundreds of entries spanning 60 years. Provides much valuable information about the many places in the lives of the Lewis brothers, with special attention given to the famous "walking tours" and holidays. As the book's cover blurb states, "Warren Lewis brings alive the subtle rhythms of English university life . . . and the reviving pleasures of the English countryside." A most welcome addition to the Lewis traveler's library and for anyone wanting to know more about his times and places. Out of print.

Lewis, C. S. *Surprised By Joy.* Orlando FL: Harcourt, 1984. Traces Lewis' life and places from early childhood in Belfast to the time of his conversion to theism (belief in God) at Oxford in 1929. A classic work of great importance to anyone interested in the psychology of conversion. A compelling personal memoir. Delightful reading. Perhaps the first book for a traveler to Lewis sites to purchase.

Neimark, Anne E. *Myth Maker: J. R. R. Tolkien.* Orlando FL: Harcourt, 1996.

Sayer, George. *Jack: A Life of C. S. Lewis.* Wheaton IL: Crossway, 1994. The best biography of Lewis, written by his friend and former student. Contains many warm and well-written references to the key places in Lewis' life, with exceptionally good sections on his boyhood home, Little Lea, and his home in Oxford, the Kilns. Available in paperback and unabridged audiotape (Blackstone Audio Books: Ashland OR).

Sibley, Brian. *C. S. Lewis Through the Shadowlands.* Grand Rapids MI: Revell, 1994. A good biography of C. S. Lewis and Joy Gresham. Contains the usual references to Lewis' places, especially in Oxford. Available in paperback.

Tolkien, John and Priscilla. *The Tolkien Family Album.* Boston: Houghton Mifflin, 1992. A charming and loving "informal portrait" of the Tolkien family, written by J. R. R. Tolkien's only daughter and eldest son. Includes an overview of Tolkien's life with Edith Bratt, his horrific World War I experiences, the birth of his 4 children, his academic career, and the writing of the works of fantasy that have sold millions of copies worldwide and made him a household name. Contains many photos from the family's own picture albums and letters, some unique to this book. Valuable for the visitor to Oxford who wants to know more about Tolkien's places. Informative pictures and comments about Tolkien's homes, colleges, and churches.

Vanauken, Sheldon. *A Severe Mercy*. New York: Harper, 1987. A celebrated and bestselling memoir tracing the idyllic marriage of Sheldon and Jean Vanauken, their search for faith, their friendship with C. S. Lewis, and the tragedy of Davy's untimely death. Set mostly in Oxford in the 1950s. Includes 18 letters from Lewis and much information about the times and places of the Vanaukens. Available in paperback and unabridged audiotape (North Star Audio Books, Van Wyck SC).

Wellman, Sam *C. S. Lewis*. Uhrichsville OH: Barbour, 1997.

Wilson, A. N. *C. S. Lewis: A Biography*. New York: Norton, 1990. Highly publicized and well written, but mean-spirited and teeming with inaccuracies and half-truths. Contains many references to the places in Lewis' life, including a good section on Lewis' boyhood and homes in Belfast. Available in paperback.

Ireland, Belfast, Oxford, Cambridge, England

Bardon, Jonathan, and David Burnett. *Belfast: A Pocket History*. Belfast: The Blackstaff Press, 1996. A concise and reliable history of Belfast from its beginnings as a base for Presbyterian settlement to its current status as a shipping and industrial center. Contains some information about Lewis sites such as the Queen's University, Campbell College, and the Royal Belfast Academical Institution.

Bell, Brian, ed. *Insight City Guides—Oxford*. London: APA Publications, 1990. The most popular and bestselling guide to the history, places, and people of Oxford. Beautiful color plates and detailed descriptions. $20.

Crosher, G. R. *Along the Cotswold Ways.* London: Cassell, 1976. An older introduction to the Cotswolds. Explores "unknown" parts of the countryside Lewis loved: the upland fields, remote farms, and secretive tracks. The chapter on Cotswold churches would delight even Lewis. It is a gold mine of little known facts, lore, and history.

De-la-Noy, Michael. *Exploring Oxford.* London: Headline House, 1992. One of the best guides to Oxford. Contains detailed descriptions of 10 walks through the city's colleges, chapels, thoroughfares, pubs, and meadows. A chapter describes Magdalen College, its deer park, and the St. Cross Church cemetery, where several of Lewis' friends are buried, including Charles Williams, Austin Farrer, and Hugo Dyson.

Dowey, Mary. *The Best of Belfast.* Belfast: A. & A. Farmar, 1996. An excellent guide for traveling around Belfast, with exceptionally good maps and directions.

Duncan, Andrew. *Oxford.* London: New Holland, 1989. Contains excellent photography, including a beautiful color cover picture of Magdalen College New Buildings where Lewis resided and gave tutorials, and descriptions of major places of interest in Oxford, many of which Lewis visited.

Hall, Michael. *Oxford.* Englewood Cliffs NJ: Prentice Hall, 1983. Popular with Oxford enthusiasts. Part of the best-selling series "Color Guides to Great Britain." Contains a wealth of information, including history, pictures, and descriptions of the colleges of the University of Oxford. With its companion volume, *Cambridge* (1983), is an excellent guide for the beginning traveler to Lewis' universities.

Hannah, Jean. *Coping with England.* Oxford: Blackwell, 1987. An invaluable guide for the first-time visitor to Lewis' England. Filled with easy-to-read information about travel, accommodations, recreation, shopping, the English way of talking, and much more. Contains information to help the visitor understand the customs and patterns of everyday life in England. Not specifically about Lewis' places, but will greatly benefit the Lewis visitor in "coping well" with England.

Killinger, John. *Oh, To Be in England!* Centreville VA: Plain Vanilla Press, 1996. A warm and interesting introduction and memoir. Includes a good chapter on Oxford and Cambridge. Gives a 1-week and a 2-week sample tour to England.

Morris, Jan. *Oxford.* Oxford: Oxford University Press, 1991. A superlative work by a renowned travel narrative writer. Explores the history, lore, people, and architecture of the "city of dreaming spires." Indispensable for the Lewis traveler to Oxford. Available in paperback.

Sale, Richard. *Visitor's Guide—Cotswolds* (4th ed.). Edison NJ: Hunter Publishing, 1995. Written with the independent traveler in mind. Contains a wealth of information and pictures and maps about an area of England that Lewis loved to visit.

Snelling, Rebecca, ed. *Town and City Guides—Cambridge.* Basingstoke, Hampshire, England: Automobile Association, 1988. Contains many descriptions of the colleges and major places of interest in Cambridge, complete with maps and street plans. Designed for the visitor who wants to take walking and motor tours.

Tan, Terry. *Culture Shock! Britain.* Portland OR: Graphic Arts Publishing, 1992. Similar in type to Hannah's *Coping with England.*

Taylor, Kevin. *Central Cambridge—A Guide to the University and Colleges.* Cambridge: Cambridge University Press, 1994. Provides information on "walking tours" of Cambridge. Contains excellent maps of the city and colleges, including one of Lewis' Magdalene College.

Tyack, Geoffrey. *Blue Guide—Oxford and Cambridge.* New York: Norton, 1995. Part of the Blue Guide travel series begun in 1915. Details the history, architecture, and lore of the colleges in Oxford and Cambridge. Includes good maps and instructions on "how to get there." Features many Lewis sites in both cities.

Weisser, Henry. *The Hippocrene Companion Guide to Ireland*. New York: Hippocrene Books, 1994. A concise overview of the culture, society, politics, and history of the Emerald Isle. A primer designed to prepare the traveler for Ireland. Also recommended are *The Hippocrene Companion Guide to Britain* (1993) and *The Hippocrene Language and Travel Guide to Britain* (1995).

Other

Frank, Bryn. *Short Walks in English Towns*. New York: Harmony Books, 1988. Companion volume to *Book of British Villages*. Describes walks through Oxford and Cambridge. Includes excellent 3-D maps.

Hibbert, Christopher. *The Encyclopedia of Oxford*. London: Papermac, 1988. Contains much valuable information about Lewis' colleges, pubs, churches, and so on. Contributors include Humphrey Carpenter, author of *The Inklings* and *Tolkien*, and Peter Bayley, Lewis' former student.

Snow, Peter. *Oxford Observed*. London: John Murray, 1992. A readable and interesting "tell it like it is" guide to the Oxford of the 1990s.

The Oxford Handbook (Oxford University Student Union) and *Cambridge Through Student Eyes* (Varsity Publications). On arriving in Lewis' Oxford and Cambridge, the visitor should try to obtain these student publications. Entertaining. Published yearly.

The *Book of British Villages*. England: Reader's Digest Association, 1985. Contains much information in a beautiful format about some of the villages and towns Lewis visited, especially in the Cotswolds.

"The C. S. Lewis Trail." A free brochure that contains information, pictures, maps, and suggested tours of Lewis' places in Belfast and Country Down. Available from C. S. Lewis Centenary Group, 11 Raglan Road, Bangor, County Down, BT20 3TL, Northern Ireland.

Maps

1998 RAC Road Atlas—Britain (RAC Publishing).

EuroAtlas—Great Britain: England, Wales, Scotland, Ireland (American Map Corporation).

Greater Belfast Street Map (Ordinance Survey of Northern Ireland).

Glovebox Atlas—Ireland (Automobile Association, England).

Ireland—North (Ordinance Survey, England).

Street AZ Plan—Oxford (Geographers' A-Z Map Company).

Street AZ Plan—Cambridge (Geographers' A-Z Map Company).

The Cotswolds (Ordinance Survey Touring Map & Guide 8, England).

Suggested Tours

8 Days

DAY 1—
- Arrive at London's Gatwick Airport.
- Take a 2-hour guided double-decker bus tour of London.
- Take a bus trip to Malvern, where Lewis lived.
- Check in early at a hotel or bed & breakfast.

DAY 2—
- Visit Cherbourg School (now called "Ellerslie") and Malvern College.
- Tour Malvern Hills.
- Visit historic Priory Church.
- Stay overnight.

DAY 3—
- Depart Malvern early by bus or train to Oxford.
- Check into the Eastgate Hotel where Lewis first met Joy Gresham.
- Tour Botanic Garden, where Lewis and Tolkien walked, and Christ Church Meadows.
- Tour Christ Church College and Cathedral.
- Sightsee and shop in downtown Oxford.

DAY 4—
- Eat an early lunch at the Eagle and Child pub where Lewis and the Inklings met.
- Tour Magdalen College. Stroll around Addison's Walk where Lewis was converted.
- Visit the chapel where part of *Shadowlands* was filmed.
- Visit St. Mary's University Church where Lewis preached the sermon "The Weight of Glory."
- Have dinner at the Checquers pub, one of Lewis' favorites.

DAY 5—
- Visit Headington; see the homes of J. R. R. Tolkien and Joy Gresham.
- Visit the Kilns.
- Visit Holy Trinity Church, Lewis' home church and gravesite.
- Spend an afternoon in the Ashmolean Museum.
- Have dinner at the Eastgate Hotel.

DAY 6—
- Depart early for a 3-hour bus trip to Cambridge.
- Tour Magdalene College, including Fellows' Garden where Lewis walked and the chapel where he preached his last sermon.
- Sightsee in the city centre.

DAY 7—
- Visit King's College Chapel.
- Visit Round Church and Great St. Mary's Church where Lewis worshiped.
- Eat lunch at the Blue Boar Inn.
- See Mill Lane lecture hall where Lewis gave his famous inaugural address, "De Descriptione Temporum."
- Visit medieval colleges and walk the "Backs" where Lewis often walked.

DAY 8—
- Depart early by train for London.
- See Buckingham Palace and other royal places.
- Visit famous bookshops on Charing Cross Road.
- Check in early at a hotel or bed & breakfast; prepare for the trip home.

13 Days

DAY 1—
- Arrive at London's Gatwick Airport.
- Take a 2-hour double-decker bus tour of city.
- Travel by tube (underground) to Northampton and St. Matthew's Church where Lewis preached the sermon "Miserable Offenders."
- Shop and sightsee.

DAY 2—
- Depart London early for Belfast International Airport.
- Travel to Crawfordsburn (about 25 miles from the Belfast city centre) and stay at the Old Inn, where Lewis stayed with Joy.
- Find the Silver Hill area and 21 Ballymullan Road where Lewis' friend Arthur Greeves lived.
- Visit Crawfordsburn Country Park.
- Visit St. John's in nearby Helen's Bay, where Lewis worshiped.

DAY 3—
- Travel south to northeast Belfast.
- Tour Lewis sites in the Strandtown district: his boyhood home "Little Lea" on Circular Road, Arthur Greeves' home "Bernagh" (now a nursing home, "Red Hall") across the street, Lewis' home church St. Mark's on Holywood Road, and Campbell College (Lewis attended in 1910) off Belmont Road.

DAY 4—
- Sightsee and shop in central Belfast.
- Visit the Harland and Wolff shipbuilding company on Belfast Lough where the *Titanic* was built.
- Enjoy scenery near the Old Inn, especially the beaches.

DAY 5—
- Depart early for London.
- Take a 2-hour bus or 1-hour train trip to Oxford.
- Check in at the Eastgate Hotel where Lewis met his wife Joy for the first time.
- Tour Botanic Garden where Lewis and Tolkien walked.
- Visit Christ Church Meadows, College, and Cathedral. (Ask the guide for a look out a door marked "private" on the right [front] side of the church facing the chancel. This leads to a private garden where Lewis Carroll [*Alice in Wonderland*] met Alice and her friends.)
- Have dinner at the Eastgate Hotel.

DAY 6—

- Visit the Eagle and Child pub in downtown Oxford at 11 A.M. (opening time) and see the "Rabbit Room" where Lewis and the Inklings met.
- Tour Lewis' bookshops: Blackwell's, Thornton's, Waterfield's.
- Visit Keble College where Lewis' friend Austin Farrer taught and preached; see the chapel and its small prayer room where Holman Hunt's famous painting *The Light of the World* hangs.
- Sightsee and shop in central Oxford.

DAY 7—

- Rise early.
- Visit St. Mary's University Church on High Street where Lewis preached the sermon "The Weight of Glory" and where John Wesley also preached. Spend time in the church's coffee shop (in a 300-year-old room). Take pictures of the Radcliffe Camera reading room behind the church. Visit the Bodleian Library's gift shop. Take the Divinity School tour.
- Visit Sheldonian Theatre where Lewis matriculated.
- Take a break at the King's Arms or Lamb and Flag pubs where Lewis visited often.
- Go to the Trout Inn at Godstow (one of Lewis' favorite places). See Joy Lewis' famous memorial at the Oxford Crematorium. Relax outside by the river where Lewis Carroll read his stories and Evelyn Waugh often entertained guests.

DAY 8—

- Rise early for a bus tour from downtown Oxford of the lovely Cotswolds, where Lewis and friends visited often.
- Eat lunch at the Mitre (arrive any time but noon).
- Visit Oxford's Covered Market.
- Travel to Headington and visit the Kilns and Holy Trinity church.
- Have dinner at the Studley Priory Hotel where Lewis and his wife Joy visited often.

DAY 9—
- Rise early.
- Visit the Bookshop-on-the-Plain (a small "hidden treasure") near Magdalen College.
- Cross Magdalen Bridge to the College and see the chapel where part of *Shadowlands* was filmed.
- Stroll around the medieval cloisters to New Buildings where Lewis lived, met students for tutorials, and hosted Inklings meetings.
- Tour Addison's Walk where Lewis was convinced of the truth of the Christian faith.
- Visit St. Mary's Church.
- Relax and sightsee.
- Visit Ashmolean Museum.
- Have dinner at the Eastgate Hotel.

DAY 10—
- Rise early for a 3-hour bus trip or 2-hour train trip to Cambridge.
- Eat lunch at the Pickerell Inn.
- Visit Magdalene College and chapel where Lewis preached his last sermon and where he prayed every day "in term."
- Visit Pepys Library.
- Walk around Fellows' Gardens where Lewis often strolled.
- Sightsee and shop in central Cambridge.

DAY 11—
- Rise early.
- Walk around Cambridge's "Backs" behind the colleges on the river Cam.
- Visit King's College Chapel.
- Tour Round Church.
- Eat lunch at Vivat Brassiere, an intimate basement restaurant.
- Visit the Haunted Bookshop in St. Edward's Passage.
- Visit Great St. Mary's Church where Lewis worshiped.
- Relax with tea and cakes at Henry's on Pembroke (also sells teapots and "tea accessories").
- Visit Mill Lane lecture hall where Lewis gave his inaugural address "De Descriptione Temporum."

DAY 12—

- At mid-morning walk to Grantchester and Newnham. Find Byron's Pool and the clearing where the lamp-post stands that is perhaps the model for the one in the Narnian stories.
- Visit the shops in Grantchester.
- See the poet Rupert Brooke's homes the Old Vicarage and the Orchard.
- Visit Trinity Hall and its library grounds, called by Henry James "the prettiest corner in the world."
- Visit Trinity College's Great Court (the largest college court in either Oxford or Cambridge, and the original scene of the "Great Court Run" featured in the movie *Chariots of Fire*).

DAY 13—

- Travel to London via bus or train.
- Tour St. Paul's Cathedral where the Lewis brothers visited in 1934.
- Sightsee, shop, and prepare for the trip home.

Not to Scale

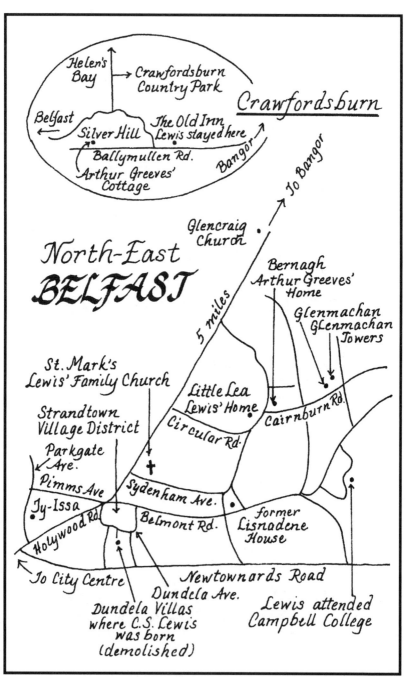

Not to Scale

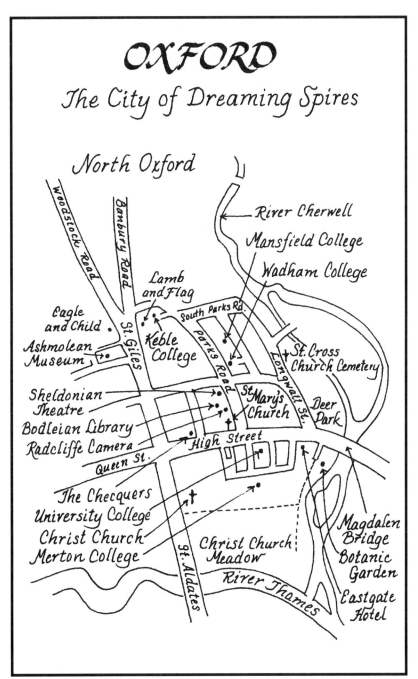

OXFORD
The City of Dreaming Spires

Not to Scale

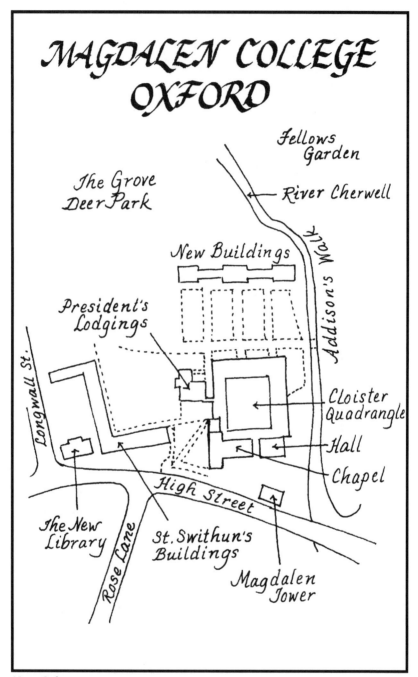

Not to Scale

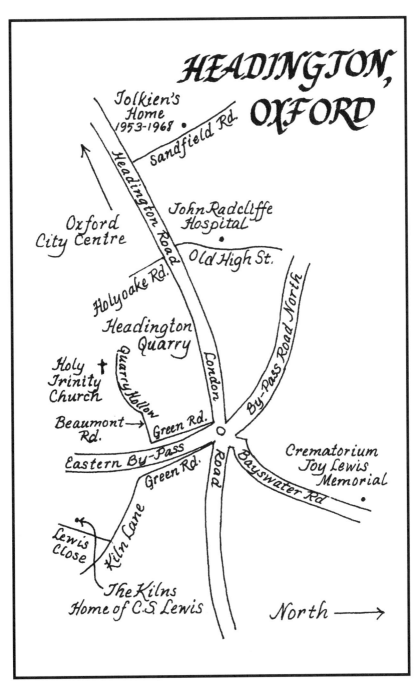

HEADINGTON, OXFORD

Tolkien's Home 1953-1968

Sandfield Rd.

Headington Road

Oxford City Centre

John Radcliffe Hospital

Old High St.

Holyoake Rd.

Headington Quarry

Holy Trinity Church

Quarry Hollow

London

By-Pass Road North

Beaumont Rd.

Green Rd.

Eastern By-Pass

Green Rd.

Road

Bayswater Rd

Crematorium Joy Lewis Memorial

Kiln Lane

Lewis Close

The Kilns Home of C.S. Lewis

North →

Not to Scale

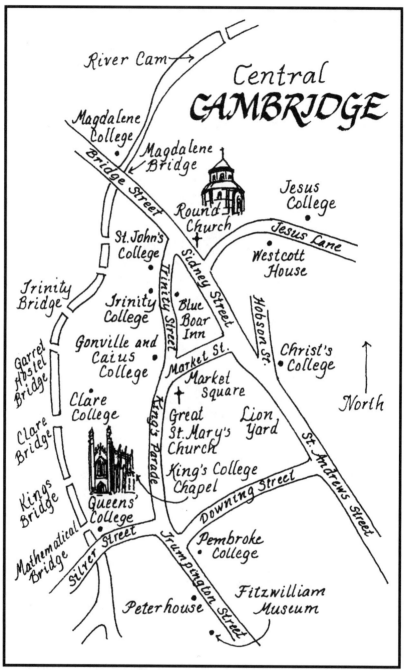

Central
CAMBRIDGE

River Cam →

Magdalene College

Magdalene Bridge

Bridge Street

Round Church

Jesus College

Jesus Lane

St. John's College

Westcott House

Trinity Bridge

Trinity College

Trinity Street

Sidney Street

Blue Boar Inn

Hobson St.

Christ's College

Garret Hostel Bridge

Gonville and Caius College

Market St.

Market Square

North

Clare College

King's Parade

Great St. Mary's Church

Lion Yard

Clare Bridge

King's College Chapel

Downing Street

St. Andrews Street

Kings Bridge

Queens' College

Mathematical Bridge

Silver Street

Trumpington Street

Pembroke College

Peterhouse

Fitzwilliam Museum

Not to Scale

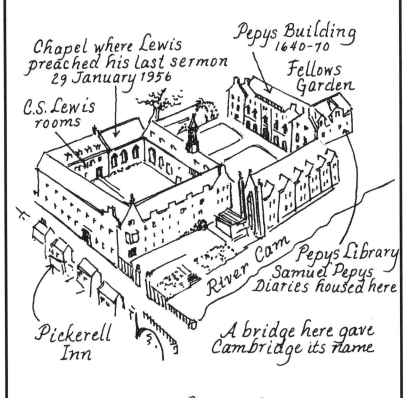

MAGDALENE COLLEGE CAMBRIDGE

Founded in 1542 as a centre of study for Benedictine monks from Crowland Abbey

Chapel where Lewis preached his last sermon 29 January 1956

Pepys Building 1640-70

Fellows Garden

C.S. Lewis rooms

River Cam

Pepys Library
Samuel Pepys Diaries housed here

Pickerell Inn

A bridge here gave Cambridge its name

C. S. Lewis was here as Professor of Medieval and Renaissance Literature 1955 – 1963

Not to Scale

Not to Scale